ESSAYS ON THE ARISTOTELIAN TRADITION

During most of the Christian millennia Aristotle has been the most influential of all philosophers. This selection of essays by the eminent philosopher and Aristotle scholar Anthony Kenny traces this influence through the ages. Particular attention is given to Aristotle's ethics and philosophy of mind, showing how they provided the framework for much fruitful development in the Middle Ages and again in the present century. Also included are some contributions to the most recent form of Aristotelian scholarship, computer-assisted stylometry. All who work on Aristotle and his intellectual legacy will find much to interest them in these *Essays on the Aristotelian Tradition*.

Essays on the Aristotelian Tradition

Anthony Kenny

CLARENDON PRESS · OXFORD
2001

OXFORD

UNIVERSITY PRESS

Great Clarendon Street, Oxford OX2 6DP
Oxford University Press is a department of the University of Oxford.
It furthers the University's objective of excellence in research, scholarship,
and education by publishing woldwide in

Oxford New York

Athens Auckland Bangkok Bogotá Buenos Aires Calcutta
Cape Town Chennai Dar es Salaam Delhi Florence Hong Kong Istanbul
Karachi Kuala Lumpur Madrid Melbourne Mexico City Mumbai
Nairobi Paris São Paulo Shanghai Singapore Taipei Tokyo Toronto Warsaw
and associated companies in Berlin Ibadan

Oxford is a registered trade mark of Oxford University Press
in the UK and certain other countries

Published in the United States
by Oxford University Press Inc., New York
© In this collection, Sir Anthony Kenny 2000

British Library Cataloguing in Publication Data
Data available.

Library of Congress Cataloging in Publication Data
Kenny, Anthony John Patrick.
Essays on the Aristotelian tradition/Anthony Kenny.
p. cm.
Includes bibliographical references and index.
1. Aristotle—Ethics. 2. Ethics, Ancient. 3. Aristotle—Contributions in philosophy of
mind. 4. Philosophy of mind—History. I. Title.
B491.E7K 49 2001   185—dc21   00–060669
ISBN 0–19–825068–1

1 3 5 7 9 10 8 6 4 2

Typeset by Kolam Information Services Pvt Ltd, Pondicherry, India
Printed in Great Britain
on acid-free paper by
TJ. International Ltd
Padstow, Cornwall

Preface

In this volume I have collected a number of essays, mainly written during the 1990s, on topics related to the Aristotelian tradition in philosophy (a tradition whose main elements I describe in the introductory chapter). The essays fall into three classes, those concerned with moral philosophy, those concerned with philosophy of mind, and those concerned with twentieth-century developments in the tradition, specifically the fortunes of the Aristotelian-Thomist revival in the Catholic Church, and the employment of stylometric methods in the study of Aristotelian texts. I have grouped the essays by subject-matter rather than by chronological order of publication. All the essays except for the introduction have been previously published.

'The Nicomachean Conception of Happiness' was published in *Aristotle and the Later Tradition* (1991), a supplementary volume of *Oxford Studies in Ancient Philosophy* edited by Henry Blumenthal and Howard Robinson as a tribute to A. C. Lloyd. The ideas in this paper were further developed in chapters 1–3 of my *Aristotle on the Perfect Life* (Clarendon Press, 1992). 'Aquinas on Aristotelian Happiness' appeared in *Aquinas's Moral Theory: Essays in Honor of Norman Kretzmann*, ed. Scott MacDonald and Eleonore Stump (Cornell University Press, 1999). 'The Principle of Double Effect' was published as 'Philippa Foot on Double Effect' in *Virtues and Reasons: Philippa Foot and Moral Theory*, ed. Rosalind Hursthouse, Gavin Lawrence, and Warren Quinn (Clarendon Press, 1995).

'The Geography of the Mind' was the first of three centenary Gifford Lectures on the Kingdom of the Mind given in Glasgow and published in *Humanity, Environment and God*, ed. Neil Spurway (Blackwell, 1993). 'Body, Soul and Intellect in Aquinas', a lecture in a series at Wolfson College, Oxford, in 1997, first appeared in *From Soul to Self*, ed. James Crabbe (Routledge 1999). 'Duns Scotus on Freewill' was read as a paper with the title 'Scotus and the Sea Battle' to a conference in Cambridge in 1994 and was published in the proceedings of that conference,

Aristotle in Britain during the Middle Ages, ed. John Marenbon (Brepols 1996). 'Aristotle versus Descartes on Sensation' was published as 'Descartes the Dualist' in the journal *Ratio*, 12 (June 1999).

'The Thomism of Pope John Paul II' appeared as a review of the Pope's encyclical letter *Fides et Ratio* in the *Tablet* of 26 June 1999. 'The Stylometric Study of the Aristotelian Writings' was published in *CIRPHO* (Autumn 1976). 'A Stylometric comparison between Five Disputed Works and the Remainder of the Aristotelian Corpus' was a paper delivered at the ninth Symposium Aristotelicum in Berlin 1981 and published in *Zweifelhaftes im Corpus Aristotelicum*, ed. Paul Moraux and Jürgen Wiesner (De Gruyter, 1983).

All the essays are reprinted as originally published, except for the removal of misprints, factual errors, and references to the original context of publication.

A.K.

Oxford
31 December 1999

Contents

1

Introduction:
The Aristotelian Tradition

I

'The European tradition in philosophy', A. N. Whitehead said famously, 'consists of a series of footnotes to Plato'. But for much of the Christian millennia the philosophical influence of Aristotle was greater than that of Plato. To be sure Aristotle himself owed an enormous debt to Plato, and he showed his influence in almost everything he wrote. But in philosophy his scope was broader and his judgement sounder than that of his master, and it would be absurd to see him only as the first and greatest of history's footnotes.

It was long traditional to regard the Academy and the Lyceum as two opposite poles of philosophy, one idealistic, Utopian, other-worldly, the other realistic, utilitarian, commonsensical. Thus, in Raphael's *School of Athens* Plato, wearing the colours of the volatile elements air and fire, points heavenwards; Aristotle, clothed in watery blue and earthy green, has his feet firmly on the ground. Many people, like Coleridge, have seen Platonists and Aristotelians as two different and irreconcilable classes of men. In fact Aristotle took a large part of his philosophical agenda from Plato, and his teaching was often more a modification than a refutation of Platonic doctrines. Modern historians have been less perceptive than the many commentators in late antiquity who saw it as their duty to construct a harmonious concord between the two greatest philosophers of the ancient world.

For centuries, however, it was largely through Aristotle's writings that Plato's ideas were handed on in the philosophical tradition. In antiquity and in the Byzantine era even Platonists often expressed their views through the medium of commentaries on

Aristotelian texts. In the Latin west in the second half of the first millennium it was largely through the works of Augustine that Platonic and classical philosophical ideas were handed on; but from the tenth until the twelfth century philosophy was most at home in the Muslim lands where Avicenna, Averroes, and Maimonides made their names as interpreters of Aristotle, whom the latter proclaimed as 'the summit of human intelligence'. Averroes' voluminous commentaries mediated to the Latin Middle Ages the works of the man who was henceforth to be known as 'The Philosopher' *par excellence*.

At the beginning of the millennium the only works of Aristotle available in Latin were a couple of basic logical treatises. Towards the end of the twelfth century, translations from Greek or Arabic appeared of all his works on logic, physics, biology, psychology, metaphysics, and ethics. Initially these products of Greek paganism, gift-wrapped in Muslim commentary, were regarded with suspicion by Christian authorities: the University of Paris, with papal backing, forbade lectures on Aristotle's natural philosophy and ordered his works to be burnt. But these condemnations were soon a dead letter, and the Aristotelian texts came to provide the canon and define the syllabus of the faculty of Arts. Thus, psychology would be studied through lectures and commentaries on the *De Anima*, physics or 'natural philosophy' through working on the text of the *Physics* or *De Generatione et Corruptione*, and so on.

The person who, more than anyone else, made Aristotle respectable in the Latin Middle Ages was Thomas Aquinas. By making a distinction between matters of faith, which can be learnt only through a divine revelation such as the Bible, and matters of philosophy, which can be reached by the unaided operation of the human reason, Aquinas achieved a working relationship between Aristotelianism and Christianity.

Aquinas wrote lengthy commentaries on Aristotle's works; he was not only a most perceptive commentator on the works of Aristotle, but in his own right an original thinker of great power. Though his principal philosophical themes and techniques are Aristotelian, he was no more a mere echo of Aristotle than Aristotle was of Plato. In addition to working out the relationship between Aristotelianism and Christianity, Aquinas develops and modifies Aristotle's ideas within the area of philosophy itself.

While he was the greatest figure in the Aristotelian tradition he cannot be thought of as belonging to an Aristotelian school. In the third essay of this book I have tried to illustrate, in a particular case, the flexible way in which he adopts and adapts Aristotelian themes and tenets to suit his philosophical and theological purposes in different contexts.

Many of the disciplines to which Aristotle contributed would nowadays be thought of as sciences rather than as branches of philosophy: briefly, and anachronistically, we can say that Aristotle was a great scientist as well as a great philosopher. He can indeed claim to have been the founder of several of the life sciences, and some of his zoological observations remained impressive until the time of Darwin. But in the Middle Ages, while the reception of his works was a great boon to philosophy, the influence of his scientific works was damaging to science. Many medieval Aristotelians took Aristotle's writings as the last as well as the first word on scientific matters, instead of following his own example of close examination of nature. His authority kept fundamental science static for much of the Middle Ages, and since the era of Bacon, Galileo, and Newton the Aristotelian tradition in natural philosophy has been effectively dead.

It is true that a number of the leading concepts of Aristotle's *Physics* retain their interest as an analysis of the ordinary use of language. The doctrine of matter and form, for instance, is a philosophical account of certain concepts which we employ in our everyday description and manipulation of material substances. Even if we grant that the account is philosophically correct, it is still a question whether the concepts which it seeks to clarify have any part to play in a scientific explanation of the universe. It is notorious that what in the kitchen appears as a substantial change of macroscopic entities may in the laboratory appear as an accidental change of microscopic entities. It remains a matter of opinion whether a notion such as that of prime matter has any application to physics at a fundamental level, where we talk of transitions between matter and energy.

In other areas of philosophy, however, the Aristotelian tradition survived much longer and in some it is still alive and fertile. The discipline of logic was Aristotle's invention: his work was subsumed, rather than superseded, by the development of mathematical logic at the end of the nineteenth century by Frege and his contemporaries. Many of the topics treated in Aristotle's metaphysical works are now discussed under the heading 'philosophy of language'. Those works, though mainly studied by scholars for historical purposes, contain ideas of the highest interest about the nature of language, the nature of reality, and the relationship between the two. In particular, the Aristotelian notion of substance still deserves an important role in any plausible semantics or epistemology. On the other hand, since Frege and Russell showed the philosophical importance of the use of the existential quantifier, it is difficult to take at face value everything to be found in Aristotle and Aquinas on the topic of Being. In general, Aristotle's contributions in all these areas of philosophy have been placed in a radically different context by recent work in the philosophy of language, especially that of Wittgenstein.

The position is quite different when we turn to moral philosophy and philosophy of mind. Here we find serious contemporary works of systematic philosophy being written by authors who are directly inspired by the writings of Aristotle and his medieval followers and who place themselves explicitly within an Aristotelian tradition. It is within these areas that most of the essays in the present volume are situated.

II

We possess Aristotle's moral philosophy in three different versions, two of them very likely his own notes for lecturing, and the third more probably notes of his lectures made by a pupil. The dating of the two authentic treatises, the *Eudemian* and *Nicomachean Ethics*, is a matter of controversy; most scholars, for no good reason, regard the *Eudemian Ethics* as a youthful and inferior work. There is much better reason for the consensus that the third work, the *Magna Moralia*, is not from Aristotle's own hand. Whatever its intrinsic merits, the *Eudemian Ethics* has never been studied by more than a handful of scholars; it is the *Nicomachean Ethics* which, since the beginning of the Christian era, has been regarded as *the* Ethics of Aristotle, and it is this work which had been dominant in the Aristotelian tradition in moral philosophy.

Both treatises give an overarching role in ethics to the concept of *eudaimonia* or happiness. When we ask for the why and wherefore of any human action, we can be told that it is to be done for the sake of something else; we can ask in turn for the why and wherefore of that something else; when we reach a point where there is no further answer to the question, we have reached the 'wherefore in the sense of end'. It is the worthwhileness of the end of an action which makes the actions leading to it themselves worthwhile: in this sense an end is the cause of the goodness of the means to it. The best of all human goods, then, would be a good which appeared at the top end of every chain of practical reasoning: that would be an absolute good, an independent good on which the goodness of every other human good depended, as the goodness of health-producing drugs or regimes depends on the goodness of health itself. This supreme good is the subject-matter of the supreme science of ethics and the virtue of wisdom: happiness, the best of human goods.

The second essay in this book summarizes the concept of happiness expounded in the *Nicomachean Ethics*; I have developed some of the ideas in this essay more fully in my book *Aristotle and the Perfect Life* (Clarendon Press, 1992). The third essay shows the different uses to which Aquinas put this concept in his own ethical system. Admirers of Aristotle have in general been more impressed with the general abstract framework of his ethics than with its detailed content, which bears the mark of the pagan Greek cultural milieu in which he wrote. Hence, Aristotle's treatment of such notions as happiness, virtue, and choice have received much more attention than his description of individual character traits such as magnanimity and wittiness. This has been true both of the Christian Middle Ages and of our own more secular period.

Aquinas's ethical system is most copiously set out in the Second Part of his *Summa Theologiae*. This work, which is nearly 900,000 words long, is always subdivided into a first part (the *Prima Secundae*) which contains the General Part of ethics, and the second part (the *Secunda Secundae*) which contains detailed teaching on individual moral topics. The work, in both structure and content, is modelled on the *Nicomachean Ethics*, on which he was, at roughly the same time, writing a line-by-line commentary.

Much in Aristotle was very congenial. Like Aristotle Aquinas identified the ultimate goal of human life with happiness, and like him he thought that happiness cannot be equated with pleasure, riches, honour, or any bodily good, but must consist in activity in accordance with virtue, especially intellectual virtue. The intellectual activity which satisfies the Aristotelian requirements for happiness is to be found perfectly only in contemplation of the essence of God; happiness in the ordinary conditions of the present life must remain imperfect. True happiness, then, even on Aristotle's terms, is to be found only in the souls of the blessed in heaven. The saints will in due course receive a bonus of happiness, undreamt of by Aristotle, in the resurrection of their bodies in glory. Aquinas expounded and improved upon Aristotle's account of virtue, action, and emotion before going on to relate these teachings to the specifically theological topics of divine law and divine grace.

In particular, Aquinas's lengthy discussion of human action marked a great advance on Aristotle or any previous Christian thinker. Aristotle had introduced the concept of voluntariness: something was voluntary if it was originated by an agent free from compulsion or error. In his moral system an important role was also played by the concept of *prohairesis* or purposive choice: this was the choice of an action as part of an overall plan of life. Aristotle's concept of the voluntary was too clumsily defined, and his concept of *prohairesis* too narrowly defined, to demarcate the everyday moral choices which make up our life. (The fact that there is no English word corresponding to *prohairesis* is itself a mark of the awkwardness of the concept; most of Aristotle's moral terminology has been incorporated into all European languages.) While retaining Aristotle's concepts, Aquinas introduced a new one of *intention*, which filled the gap left between the two of them, and greatly facilitated moral thinking.

In Aquinas's system there are three types of action. There are those things which we do for their own sake, wanted as ends in themselves: the pursuit of philosophy, for instance. There are those things which we do because they are means to ends which we want for themselves: taking medicine for the sake of our health is Aquinas's example. It is in these actions that we exhibit intention: we intend to achieve the end by the means. Finally, there are the (perhaps unwanted) consequences and side-effects which our intentional actions bring about. These are not intentional, but merely voluntary. Voluntariness, then, is the broadest category; whatever is intentional is voluntary, but not vice versa.

Intention itself, while covering a narrower area than voluntariness, is a broader concept than Aristotle's *prohairesis*.

Aquinas expounds the relation between intention and morality in the following manner. Human acts may be divided into kinds, some of which are good (for example, using one's own property), some bad (for example, stealing), and some indifferent (for example, walking in the country). Every individual concrete action, however, will be performed in particular circumstances with a particular purpose. For an action to be good, the kind it belongs to must not be bad, the circumstances must be appropriate, and the intention must be virtuous. If any of these elements is missing, the act is evil. Consequently, a bad intention can spoil a good act (almsgiving out of vainglory) but a good intention cannot redeem a bad act (stealing to give to the poor).

The morality of an act, Aquinas says, may be affected by its consequences. He makes a distinction between the harm which is foreseen and intended, and that which is foreseen and not intended. As an example of the former he cites the harm resulting from the actions of a murderer or thief; to illustrate the latter he says 'A man, crossing a field the more easily to fornicate, may damage what is sown in the field; knowingly, but without a mind to do any damage.' In both cases, he says, the sin is aggravated by the amount of harm done, but in the second only indirectly. A man may be punished as negligent for harm neither foreseen nor intended, if the action causing it was itself unlawful.

Aquinas applied his doctrine to homicide, and in particular to killing in self-defence. Augustine had taught that this was forbidden for a Christian; the Decretals said it was lawful to repel force with force. Aquinas says: an act may have two effects, one intended and the other beside the intention; thus, the act of a man defending himself may have two effects, one the preservation of his own life, the other the death of the attacker. Provided no more violence is used than necessary, such an act is permissible; however, it is never lawful to intend to kill another, unless one is acting on public authority, like a soldier or policeman. Aquinas's account was later developed by his followers into the famous doctrine of double effect. The fourth essay in this book is devoted to a discussion of this doctrine by one of the most perceptive of recent moral philosophers in the analytic philosophical tradition, Professor Philippa Foot.

The theory of intention and the doctrine of double effect are instances of the way in which Aquinas resolved many of the ambiguities, and filled many of the lacunae, of Aristotle's *Ethics*. To most of our contemporaries many of the detailed provisions of Aquinas's moral system are no more congenial than the specific characters held up for our admiration in Aristotle's account of the virtues. In particular, his treatment of the role of women, of serfdom, of usury, and of the individual's right to life depend on assumptions which many find difficult to share. His teaching on relations between the sexes, for instance, seems to be based on faulty biology. Aquinas accepted the Aristotelian theory that in biological generation the female merely provided nutrition for an active principle provided by the male, and the consequent view that, since like makes like, a female is an anomalous male. This view lies behind Aquinas's denunciation of contraception, which occurs in his treatment of 'the disordered emission of semen' whether by masturbation or other means (*Summa contra Gentiles*, iii. 122).

Aquinas's claim that this is a crime against humanity, second only to homicide, rests on the premiss that the sperm is an individual entity continuous with the embryo, the foetus, and the baby. In fact we now know that male and female gamete contribute equally to the genetic constitution of the eventual human being. Even though (for different reasons) we may agree with Aquinas that an embryo is not a fully human being before a certain stage of its development, it is, from then on, unlike the father's sperm, the same individual organism as the infant at birth. For Aquinas, the emission of semen in circumstances un-suitable for conception was the same kind of thing, admittedly on a minor scale, as the exposure or starvation of an individual infant. That is why he thought masturbation a poor man's version of homicide.

Aquinas's ignorance of biology therefore turns out to be one of the ancestors of the common modern opinion which places con-traception and abortion on the same moral plane. Since abortion, unlike contraception, involves the destruction of an individual human being, this is a serious error. It is an error which is equally disastrous whether it leads to the denunciation of both as serious sins or to propaganda in favour of both as fundamental rights of women.

III

Moral philosophy is closely related to philosophy of mind, and one might wonder whether the general structure of the Aristotelian ethical tradition has not been affected by developments in philosophical psychology in the way in which some of its specific principles have been antiquated by progress in empirical physiology. I would maintain, on the contrary, that philosophy of mind is the area in which the Aristotelian tradition is most relevant and vital. I have argued in my book *Aquinas on Mind* (Routledge, 1993) that the account of the human mind developed by Aquinas on an Aristotelian basis is as good a basis for a philosophical understanding of its nature as any other account currently on offer. Part III of the present book consists of essays which sketch the main elements of this account and which set out the reasons why I find it impressive.

One of the aspects of Aristotle's metaphysics which remains of permanent value is the set of distinctions which he draws under the general heading of potentiality and actuality. One type of potentiality, in his system, is matter, and the corresponding type of actuality is form. The use of the concepts of matter and form in the area of physics has already been mentioned; but a more interesting application of Aristotle's doctrine is found in his psychology, as expressed in his treatise *On the Soul*. For Aristotle it is not only human beings which have a soul, or psyche; all living beings have one, from daisies and molluscs upwards. A soul is simply a principle of life: it is the source of the characteristic activities of living beings. Different living beings have different abilities: plants can grow and reproduce, but cannot move or feel; animals perceive, and feel pleasure and pain; some but not all animals can move around; some very special animals, namely human beings, can also think and understand. Different kinds of soul are diversified by these different activities in which they find expression. The most general definition which Aristotle gives of a soul is that it is the form of an organic body.

As a form, a soul is an actuality of a particular kind. Aristotle at this point introduces a distinction between two kinds of actuality. Someone who knows no Greek is in a state of sheer potentiality with regard to the use of Greek. To learn Greek is to take a step from potentiality in the direction of actuality. But someone who has learnt Greek, but is not at a given time making use of that knowledge, is in a state both of actuality and potentiality: actuality by comparison with the initial position of ignorance, potentiality by comparison with someone actually speaking Greek. Simply knowing Greek Aristotle called 'first actuality'; currently speaking it he called 'second actuality'. He uses this distinction in his account of the soul: the soul is the first actuality of an organic body. The actual vital operations of living creatures are second actualities.

An Aristotelian soul is not, as such, a spirit. It is not, indeed, a tangible object; but that is because it is (like all first actualities) a potentiality. Knowledge of Greek is not a tangible object, either; but nor is it anything ghostly. If there are any souls which are capable, in whole or in part, of existing without a body—a point on which Aristotle found it difficult to make up his mind—disembodiment is possible not because they are souls, but because they are souls of a particular kind with specially impressive vital activities.

Aquinas's concept of mind takes as its basis the Aristotleian thesis that the soul is the form of an organic body. The intellectual soul, for him, is the unique form of a human body; and he builds his philosophy of mind around his account of the nature and operation of the human intellect. Aquinas's account of the relation between body, soul, and intellect is sketched in the sixth essay of this book, But prior to that, in the fifth essay, I draw in a more general way the contrast between the Aristotelian position and its principal rival, the Cartesian vision of the mind. For the Aristotelian, the key to grasping the nature of the mind is intellectual understanding; for the Cartesian it is consciousness as presented in experience.

Among the medieval scholastics, Duns Scotus was second only to Aquinas in intellectual power. But though he worked in the Aristotelian tradition in the philosophy of mind, he developed it in ways which were to lead to its obliteration in the early modern period. In treating of the intellect, he introduced a notion of intuitive knowledge, which was an ancestor of the Cartesian notion of consciousness; in treating of the will he introduced a radical concept of freedom which was to pave the way for scepticism and irrationalism. The seventh essay explains how he developed this concept in the context of the Aristotlian treatment of contingency and how in the course of his discussion he invented the idea of possible worlds, which was to have a long history up to the present day.

At the same time as the work of Galileo and his successors was, happily, putting an end to the Aristotelian tradition in physics, the writing of Descartes was, less happily, putting in the shade the Aristotelian tradition in philosophical psychology. The final essay in the section on philosophy of mind draws the contrast between Aristotelian hylomorphism and Cartesian dualism. Descartes's onslaught on Aristotle was so successful that many people to this day take for granted his approach to the understanding of the mind, even when (as many do) they overtly reject his dualism.

The fundamental incoherence of the Cartesian system has been exposed by Kant, and in more recent times by Wittgenstein. Many of those who have been convinced by the Kantian and Wittgensteinian refutations of Descartes have realized that the best worked out systematic alternative to Cartesianism is to be found in the Aristotelian tradition.

IV

In the twentieth century, there have been three principal styles of Aristotelian study. In Roman Catholic countries the Aristotelian system was restored to a dominant position by the encyclical letter of Pope Leo XIII which gave St Thomas Aquinas a special place in the teaching of philosophy and theology in seminaries and universities. Until the Second Vatican Council there was a lively tradition of neo-scholasticism which, in addition to producing 'Thomist' textbooks of sometimes dubious authenticity, gave the learned world scholarly editions of many of the great medieval Aristotelians. In the English-speaking world, and especially in Oxford where chosen works of Aristotle were in the twentieth century no less than in the Middle Ages a part of the core syllabus in humanities, philosophers devoted their attention to the elucidating of the sense of the texts and relating them to contemporary developments in philosophy. In Germany scholars followed a tradition started in the nineteenth century which studied Aristotle principally from a historical point of view, striving to establish the authenticity and chronology of the works handed down in the Aristotelian corpus.

My own writings on Aristotle, including the essays in this book, have been situated within the English analytical tradition; I have studied Aristotle not so much to establish his precise delinea- ments and his place in history, as to see what we can learn philosophically from the texts which have come down to us in his name. In the final section of this book, however, I have included essays which relate to the other two of the three streams of Aristotelianism which I have distinguished.

The ninth essay, on the Thomism of Pope John Paul II, reviews the Pope's encyclical *Fides et Ratio* which laments the decline of Aristotelian scholasticism since the Second Vatican Council and calls for a revival of Thomism in Catholic centres of learning. The tenth and eleventh essays relate to a comparatively recent devel- opment in the study of the structure and development of the Aristotelian corpus: namely, the statistical study of style, which has come to be known as 'stylometry'. Since the nineteenth cen- tury, studies of the chronological development of Plato have appealed—in addition to signs of philosophical maturation, and to the varying importance of Socrates in the dialogues—to a number of minute features of vocabulary, syntax, and style which differ from dialogue to dialogue. It was only in the second half of the twentieth century that similar methods began to be applied systematically to the Aristotelian corpus—with ever greater enthusiasm as the development of computer techniques and the availability of machine-readable texts simplified the task of quantitative and statistical study of the corpus.

The tenth essay represents a rather primitive venture in Aris- totelian stylometry which I undertook in the mid 1970s following the pioneering studies of A. Q. Morton, Alban Winspear, and S. Michaelson. Later in the decade I wrote a book, *The Aristotelian Ethics* (Clarendon Press, 1978) which used stylometric methods to address a particular problem of Aristotelian scholarship: the ori- ginal home of the three disputed books which appear in the manuscript tradition of both the *Nicomachean* and *Eudemian Ethics*. The conclusion which I drew, from a series of independent styl- istic studies, was that the books belonged with the *Eudemian Ethics* and that this should be taken into account in any attempt to assign a chronology to Aristotle's ethical writings. The Eudemian assignment of the disputed books seems now to be very widely accepted, though few have been willing to draw what seem to me to be the appropriate chronological conclusions. (I returned to the topic in 1992 in an appendix to *Aristotle on the Perfect Life*.)

In the early 1980s, I tried to apply stylometric methods to a much less tractable problem, the structure and chronology of the *Metaphysics*, which had much exercised scholars in the school of Werner Jaeger. It was the virtually unanimous opinion of scholars that the work was not designed as a single whole by Aristotle, but that it represented the result of editorial collection of a number of originally separate treatises of varying dates. The common opinion was that books A and B represented a comparatively early stage in the evolution of Aristotle's metaphysical thought, and that books ZHΘ, which can be read as a consecutive whole, belonged to the most mature period of his life. Book I was commonly assigned to the same period as ZHΘ, while the dating of Γ, M, and N was controversial; and Λ had been assigned both to the very earliest, and to the very latest, period of Aristotle's life. Finally, the authenticity of two of the books, α and K, was commonly questioned.

In an attempt to throw light on these problems I studied the frequency of common particles and other vocabulary features in each of the books of the *Metaphysics* in the hope of finding features which marked out the blocks on which there was a scholarly consensus, and which could then be used to study each of the contentious works with a view to seeing which of the main blocks they most resembled.

In a paper of 1982 not here reproduced ('A Stylometric Study of Aristotle's *Metaphysics*' in the *Journal of the Association of Literary and Linguistic Computing*) I presented a report on my work in progress in this area. There were a number of independent features of vocabulary usage in which there was a marked discrepancy between AB and ZHΘ, and these went some way to confirm the opinion of scholars that those two books belonged to different periods of Aristotle's development. If we take comparative resemblance to AB as an indicator of early date, and comparative resemblance to ZHΘ as an indicator of late date, then the evidence suggested that I and E were late, with ΛMN intermediate in time, with Λ much closer to the later works than to the earlier ones. No clear conclusion emerged concerning the chronological position of Γ and K, and few of the results were more than provisional.

I was never able to bring my studies of the *Metaphysics* to achieve a convincing overall conclusion with which I was satisfied; but the Symposium Aristotelicum of 1981, which was devoted to a study of dubiously authentic works, including *Metaphysics* α and K, gave me an opportunity to present some of my particular results to the world of Aristotelian scholarship. That paper, which was published in the proceedings of the Symposium, forms the final essay of the present collection.

I

Moral Philosophy in the Aristotelian Tradition

2

The Nicomachean Conception of Happiness

At the beginning of the *Nicomachean Ethics* (*NE*) we meet the following line of argument. The subject-matter of ethics is the good for man, the end of action for the sake of which all else is desired. Most people would agree that this supreme good is happiness, however much they may disagree about what precisely happiness consists in. Aristotle goes on to expand the general view that the supreme good is happiness by outlining the three traditional lives—the life of philosophy, that of virtue, and that of pleasure. He begins his own account by saying that the good we are looking for must be perfect[1] by comparison with other ends—that is, it must be something sought always for its own sake and never for the sake of anything else; and it must be self-sufficient—that is, it must be something which taken on its own makes life worthwhile and lacking in nothing.

Happiness[2] has both these properties ($1097^a15–^b21$). What then is happiness? To elucidate this we must consider the function of man. Man must have a function because particular types of men (e.g. sculptors) do, and parts and organs of human beings do. What is it? Not life, not at least the life of growth and nourishment, for this is shared by plants, nor the life of the senses, for this is shared by animals. It must be a life of reason concerned with action: the activity of the soul in accordance with reason. So the good of man will be his good functioning: the activity of soul in accordance with virtue. If there are several virtues, it will be in accordance with the best and most perfect virtue ($1097^b22–1098^a18$).

---

[1] Thus I translate the Greek word τέλειον to avoid begging the question whether in particular contexts Aristotle means by it 'complete' or 'final'.

[2] I use this translation of εὐδαιμονία because it is traditional and convenient. I am well aware that the meaning of the Greek and English words overlaps rather than coincides.

Thus far the familiar account in the *NE*. If we turn to the *Eudemian Ethics* (*EE*) we find an account which resembles this in some ways, but which also displays important differences. The most important of these is that while the *NE*, in book I, leaves open the possibility that happiness is identified with a single dominant end, namely, the activity of the highest virtue, the *EE* views happiness as an inclusive end, the activity of all the virtues of the soul—the rational soul in the broadest sense of the word. The *NE* says that the good for man is 'activity of soul in accordance with virtue, and if there are several virtues, in accordance with the best and most perfect'. In the last chapter of the book we are told that there is indeed more than one virtue—there are, for instance, moral and intellectual virtues—and hence, we conclude, unconditionally, that happiness is activity in accordance with the best and most perfect of these many virtues. In book 10 we learn that the best and most perfect virtue is understanding,[3] and its activity, contemplation, is therefore to be identified with happiness.

In the *EE* we are told that happiness is 'activity of complete life in accordance with perfect virtue', and the word 'perfect' has just been unambiguously glossed when Aristotle has said that 'life is either perfect or imperfect, and so also virtue—one being whole virtue, another a part' (1219^a35–9). So that when in the *EE* Aristotle goes on to distinguish parts of the soul and virtues, and he lists moral and intellectual virtues, we know their activities are all supposed to be parts of happiness. The virtue which figures in the definition of the end of man is the virtue constituted by several virtues of different parts of the soul.

The account just briefly enunciated I first put forward in a paper on happiness in 1966, and developed further in the course of the comparison which I undertook between the *NE* and the *EE* in my book *The Aristotelian Ethics* in 1978. In writing thus I was taking sides on a disputed question, the question whether, in the terminology introduced by W.F.R. Hardie,[4] Aristotle's conception of happiness in the *NE* was 'dominant' or 'inclusive': that is, whether he saw supreme happiness as consisting in a single

---

[3] I thus translate the Greek σοφία in preference to the traditional translation 'wisdom', which is much more appropriate as a translation of the Greek word φρόνησις.

[4] 'The Final Good in Aristotle's Ethics', *Philosophy*, 40 (1965), 277–95; also in ch. 2 of *Aristotle's Ethical Theory* (Oxford, 1968).

activity, or in the exercise of several independently valued pur-
suits. My thesis might be stated by saying that in the *NE* Aristotle
proposed a dominant view of happiness, in the *EE* an inclusive
view.

During the twenty-five years since Hardie introduced his distinction the correct interpretation of the *NE* has been a matter of
vigorous debate which shows no signs of diminishing.[5] Contri-
butors to this debate principally concentrate, as I shall in this
essay, on the interpretation of *NE* 1 and 10, and in particular on
chapter 7 of each book. Their contributions to the debate can be
crudely classified as being on one side or other of the dominant
vs. inclusive debate. For the dominant view: Kenny, Clark, Heinaman; for the inclusive view: Ackrill, Irwin, Price, Devereux.
Cooper, having in 1975 defended a qualified version of the
dominant view, in 1987 defends a nuanced form of the inclusive
view.

In my view, much the best recent treatment of the question is
that by Heinaman. Heinaman draws a number of distinctions
which clear up confusion in other writers, and allow a clear
view to be taken of the position of the *NE*. I shall begin by
introducing the distinction which Heinaman makes, and then
state my reasons for thinking his approach is the correct one.

For Aristotle, according to Heinaman, the total life of a human
being consists in a variety of types of activity, e.g. perceiving,
growing, digesting, thinking. Each of these types of activity is
called by Aristotle a 'life', and when he identifies happiness with
a certain kind of life, it is 'life' in this sense that he means, not
'total life'. When he identifies happiness with the rational life, he

---

[5] Here is a list—by no means complete—of treatments of the topic in 1965–92:
A. Kenny, 'Happiness', *Proceedings of the Aristotelian Society*, 66 (1965–6), 93–102;
J. L. Ackrill, *Aristotle on* eudaimonia (London, 1974); J. Cooper, *Reason and Human
Good in Aristotle* (Cambridge 1975); S. R. L. Clark, *Aristotle's Man* (Oxford 1975);
A. Kenny, *The Aristotelian Ethics* (Oxford, 1978); A. W. Price, 'Aristotle's Ethical
Holism', *Mind*, 89 (1980), 341–51; D. Devereux, 'Aristotle on the Essence of Happi-
ness', in D. J. O'Meara (ed.), *Studies in Aristotle* (Washington, DC, 1981), 249–60;
T. H. Irwin, *Aristotle*, Nicomachean Ethics (Indianapolis, 1985); id., 'Stoic and
Aristotelian Conceptions of Happiness', in M. Schofield and G. Striker (eds.),
The Norms of Nature (Cambridge, 1986), 205–44; J. Cooper, 'Contemplation and
Happiness, a Reconsideration', *Synthese*, 72 (1987), 187–216; R. Heinaman, 'Eudai-
monia and Self-Sufficiency in the Nicomachean Ethics', *Phronesis*, 33 (1988), 31–49;
T. D. Roche, '*Ergon and Eudaimonia* in *Nicomachean Ethics* I: Reconsidering the
Intellectualist Interpretation', *Journal of the History of Philosophy*, 26 (1988), 175–94.

is identifying it with intellectual activity, not with a certain kind of total life.

There are at least four different questions to be distinguished to which Aristotle gives different answers but which comprehensive interpreters tend to assimilate:
(1) What life is the highest kind of *eudaimonia?*
(2) What life counts as *eudaimonia?*
(3) What components will make up the total life of the happy man?
(4) What must a man have in order to be happy?

Heinaman believes that the inclusive interpretation rests on a failure to distinguish between the first three questions. He offers his own answer to these questions, all of which I believe to be correct:

The answer to (1) is contemplation.
The answer to (2) is that both contemplation and moral action do.
The answer to (3) will include a variety of activities such as, for instance, perception.
The answer to (4) will include friends, money, food and drink.

In the argument which leads to these conclusions the most important steps concern two passages in the first book of the *NE*.

At the end of the function argument we read: 'if this is the case, human good turns out to be the activity of soul which is the exercise of virtue, and if there are several virtues, in the exercise of the best and most perfect' (1098ª16–18). A number of questions arise. First, is the second half of the quoted sentence a conclusion of the function argument, or something further added? It seems more natural to take it as part of the argument, and this is one of the strong points of the inclusive interpretation. Thus, Roche argues that there is nothing in the function argument which suggests that the human good should be confined to activities which are the exercise of contemplative virtue. To reach such an intellectualist conclusion, the argument should have concluded 'the function of man is activity of soul in accordance with theoretical reason'; but of course it says nothing of the kind.[6]

However, if we are to take this section in accordance with the inclusive view, we have to translate the final part of the sentence not, as most translators do, as 'the best and most perfect among

---

[6] *'Ergon and Eudaimonia'*, 183.

them', but as Ackrill translates, 'the best and most complete virtue', that is to say, virtue which is the whole of which the individual virtues are parts.

There are several difficulties about this. It is true that the Greek word ἀρετή like the English word 'virtue' can be used as a mass-noun (as in 'a man of great virtue') or as a count-noun (as in 'a man of many virtues'), but on Ackrill's view Aristotle is made to switch from the mass-noun to the count-noun use and back again to the mass-noun use within a space of ten words.

Secondly, there is a problem about the Greek word which is translated 'perfect'. The word means literally 'endy'; in different contexts the most appropriate English version may be 'final', 'perfect', or 'complete'. As we have already seen, the sense 'complete' is the appropriate one in the parallel passages of the *EE*. But is it the appropriate one here? In its favour, it may be said that in the very next line Aristotle goes on to speak of 'a perfect life', which clearly means a complete life as opposed to a partial or interrupted one. But the relevant sense here is surely the one explained by Aristotle in setting out the preambles to the function argument at 1097ª30.

The sense is well explained by Heinaman:

If we assume that 'teleion' means the same at 1097ª30 and 1098ª19, then it can be proved that 'the most teleion' virtue at 1098ª18 cannot mean 'the most comprehensive virtue'. For Aristotle explains what he means by 'more teleion' (teleioteron) at 1097ª30–ᵇ6, and that explanation is incompatible with an interpretation of 'teleion' as meaning 'complete'.

I take 1097ª30–ᵇ6 to be saying:

x is more teleion than y if

(i) x is chosen for its own sake and y is always chosen for the sake of something else, or
(ii) x is chosen for its own sake and never for the sake of anything else, and y is chosen for its own sake and for the sake of something else.

Aristotle gives wealth as an example of an end which is chosen for the sake of something else (1097ª27) and honor as an example of something chosen for its own sake (1097ᵇ24). So honor is more teleion than wealth on Aristotle's criterion. But of course honor is not a more complete or comprehensive end than wealth. (p. 38)

Heinaman concludes that the second part of the sentence under discussion refers to perfect happiness, not just happiness, and is therefore going on to make a further point, derived not just from the function argument but also from the notion of finality. I would prefer to say that Aristotle is at this point leaving room for, rather than arguing for, the identification of contemplation with perfect happiness. It is only later that Aristotle goes on to distinguish between moral and intellectual virtues; and within intellectual virtues between wisdom and understanding. Only in book 10 are moral virtues, plus the intellectual virtue of wisdom which is interlinked with them, eliminated as constituents of the supreme happiness.

It seems to me an error to say either that in this passage 'most perfect virtue' means total virtue, or that it means intellectual virtue. Cooper, in his earlier treatment, took it in the latter sense, saying that it means a most final virtue, one that has its value entirely in itself; this, he claimed, must be the virtue of the contemplative intellect.[7]

Roche criticized Cooper in the following terms:

This interpretation must be wrong. For in the very same discussion which Cooper cites, Aristotle says that intelligence (nous) and every virtue are chosen both for themselves and for the sake of eudaimonia. Since sophia is a virtue, Aristotle cannot, without contradiction, assert that it is tele-iotate in the sense insisted on by Cooper. (p. 186)

Roche's criticism fails. All virtues are chosen for the sake of happiness (for the sake of their activities); but virtues other than understanding, according to Aristotle (1177^b3), are ones where we pursue something other than their activity for its own sake. In the case of σοφία we do not seek anything other than the contemplation which is its exercise. So that understanding can be the most perfect virtue, in the sense defined, even though the virtue of understanding is not as perfect as happiness itself (which on the intellectualist view is not understanding but the contemplation which is the exercise of understanding).

But it is not correct to say that in the passage in book 1, Aristotle is referring to understanding. Rather, he is giving a description which he will show only later, in book 10, to be uniquely satisfied by σοφία. According to the traditional view, the clause 'if there are several virtues, in accordance with the best and most perfect'

---

[7] *Reason and Human Good in Aristotle*, 100 n. 10.

keeps open a place for the eventual doctrine of *NE* 10 that happiness is the activity of the supreme virtue of understanding.

Even Ackrill, the doyen of the inclusive interpreters, does not try to deny that in *NE* 10 a dominant view of happiness is adopted. No doubt we are wise not to take it for granted that *NE* 1 and *NE* 10 were written in a single stint; but there is evidence that when *NE* 1 was written Aristotle was thinking of the topic of *NE* 10 (at 1096ª5 he refers to a later discussion of the theoretical life) and that when he wrote *NE* 10 he had in mind *NE* 1 (1177ª11, where he refers to an earlier discussion which established that happiness consisted in the exercise of virtue).

In book 10 the argument goes: if happiness is activity which is the exercise of virtue, it is reasonable that it should be activity which is the exercise of the most excellent virtue: and this will be that of the best thing in us (1177ª12–13). This is either the understanding (νοῦς) or something like it, so the activity of this in accordance with its proper virtue will be perfect happiness. What does 'perfect' mean here? If it means 'final' rather than complete, that suggests that it meant the same in the passage *NE* 1 to which reference has just been made; if it means 'complete' then again it implies that there is nothing else in happiness other than the contemplative activity of νοῦς.

Aristotle then goes on to show that theoretic contemplation possesses all the qualities which, according to book I, were, in popular opinion and in truth, properties of happiness. Thus: it is the best activity, most continous and durable, the pleasantest, the most self-sufficient; it is loved for its own sake, and therefore perfect in the sense of final (1177ª19–ᵇ24). If Aristotle underwent a spectacular change in his view of happiness between book 1 and book 10 he wrote book 10 in such a way as to cover up the change entirely.

So much for the perfection of happiness. The other property which must be considered is its self-sufficiency. Aristotle's requirement that happiness must be self-sufficient, as Heinaman says, is the main argument of those who wish to press an inclusive interpretation of *NE* 1. Aristotle lays down self-sufficiency as a formal requirement of happiness, defining the self-sufficient (τὸ αὐταρκές) as 'that which on its own makes life worthy of choice and lacking in nothing' (1097ᵇ14–15). If perfect happiness on its own makes life desirable and lacking in nothing then, so it is argued, it cannot be restricted solely to contemplation. For obviously there are all sorts of other goods which would be lacking in a life of pure contemplation.

We must distinguish two questions. Is Aristotle asking:

(1) Is the happy man self-sufficient?
(2) Is *x* by itself sufficient for happiness?

The two questions, though they may be connected, are in themselves quite distinct. Someone, for instance, who regarded love as the essence of happiness might answer the first question in the negative and the second in the affirmative. Aristotle himself does not think that a happy man is self-sufficient—he makes this plain when he discusses the question whether a happy man needs friends—but he does think that contemplation alone (provided the conditions for realizing it have been fulfilled) is sufficient to make a man happy, and he gives as a reason for identifying happiness with contemplation that the contemplative approaches self-sufficiency more closely than the pursuer of the active life (1177^a25: like the just man, the contemplative will need the necessities of life, but he will not need objects of well-doing, and he will be able to theorize alone, even though he will do it better with colleagues).

The final passage which calls for discussion is the one which immediately follows the discussion of self-sufficiency. Aristotle says that when we are looking for happiness we are looking for something which, when not added to anything else, is most choice-worthy—though clearly, if so added, more choice-worthy with even the least additional good. If happiness were meant as an inclusive end, as the sum total of goods sought for their own sake, it would be absurd to speak of goods additional to happiness. Hence, Aristotle does not consider happiness as an inclusive end—unless he means the suggestion of addition to be absurd.

Ackrill and others maintain that he does, saying that the condition—'if so added'—is a *per impossibile* condition, because happiness already contains all goods which could possibly have been added to it. The condition has been taken as an impossible one, it must be admitted, even in antiquity, when Aspasius said that happiness could not be added to other things. This was on the rather different ground that other things were means to happiness, and an end and the means to it cannot be added together to make anything more choice-worthy, with reference to a passage in *Topics* 3.[8] But the interpretation which takes the suggestion of addition seriously is much commoner among medieval comment-ators: the passage is taken in this way by Eustratius, Albertus Magnus, and Thomas Aquinas.

Those who wish to interpret book 1 in a comprehensive way have two difficult options when they come to book 10. Either—like Ackrill—they accept the intellectualist interpretation of book 10, which seems plain on the face of it; or they must implausibly explain away the intellectualism of book 10. Thus Roche:

> The first book, as I have argued, presents a concept of the *ergon* and nature of man which involves practical (and moral) elements no less than theoretical ones. So if the tenth book identifies man with his theoretical intellect, we must attribute to Aristotle a contradiction so evident that he could not possibly have failed to see it.
>
> It appears that unless one is willing to accept the idea that *NE* 10. 7–8 is a textual anomaly, the traditional intellectualist interpretation of these passages must be abandoned. The rejection of this view will require the development of a plausible inclusive end interpretation of Aristotle's discussion of the good in these chapters of the *Ethics*. (p. 194)

On the face of it, the concluding section of the *NE*, instead of offering, like the *EE*, a single life offering all the values sought by the promoters of the three traditional lives, offers us a first-class, perfect happiness, consisting of the exercise of understanding, and an alternative, second-class career consisting in the exercise of wisdom and the moral virtues. The main reason why inter-preters are motivated to reject the intellectualist position is that they do not find it credible as a piece of philosophy, and as admirers of Aristotle they are unwilling to saddle his mature ethical work with such a strange doctrine.

Devereux has argued[9] that if the contemplative lacks moral virtue, there is nothing to prevent him from being quite ruthless in pursuing his goal. For example, he may by betraying a friend gain a large sum of money and thereby assure himself years of leisure for philosophizing. What would hold him back? In my book *The Aristotelian Ethics* I took up the notion of πανουργία or cunning, as described in the *EE*.

---

[8] *Commentaria in Aristotelem Graeca*, xix. 16.

[9] In his review of Cooper, *Reason and Human Good in Aristotle*: 'Aristotle on the Active and Contemplative Lives', *Philosophy Research Archives*, 3 (1977), 834–44.

The cunning man pursues a single dominant goal and is ruthless about other values. An intemperate man who pursued pleasure, come what may, would, provided he was intelligent, provide an obvious example of a cunning man. But so, if I am right, would the man who gave himself to the single hearted and unrelenting pursuit of philosophy without regard for the moral virtues. A person who organized his life entirely with a view to the promotion of philosophical speculation would be not wise but cunning... The type of person whom many regard as the hero of the *NE*, turns out, by the standards of the *EE*, to be a vicious and ignoble character. (p. 214)

The objection may be phrased thus:[10] if Aristotle made contemplation alone a constituent of perfect happiness, then in cases where there is a conflict between the demands of moral virtue and the demands of contemplation, Aristotle must say that the agent should engage in contemplation, even if the alternative is saving his neighbour from a burning house.

This objection is thus answered by Heinaman: 'Aristotle's position is that contemplation is the best part of the total life of a person. But that does not mean that there are no other valuable elements in the total life of a person which have value–in part–independently of their contribution to contemplation' (p. 53). It is wrong to think that if perfect happiness is contemplation, then anything has value only in so far as it contributes to contemplation, and that anything is an intrinsic good only if it is a component of happiness:

Thus moral action too has intrinsic value independently of any contribution it may make to contemplation, even though it is not a component of perfect eudaimonia... In the particular case, the thing to do may well be to save one's neighbour from the burning house because in that case, as the practically wise man was able to judge, moral action was better than contemplation. (ibid.)

Others have offered different ways of absolving Aristotle from excessive intellectualism. John Cooper, in his paper of 1987, has endeavoured to draw the sting of the intellectualist passages in book 10 in the following manner. When Aristotle says that contemplation is perfect happiness, he is not saying that contemplation is the whole of happiness. He is saying that contemplation is the best part of, the fine flower of, a happiness which contains also the activity of the moral virtues.

[10] See Heinaman, 'Eudaimonia and Self-Sufficiency', 51.

But this is unconvincing. First, the account seems to be vulnerable to the arguments of an earlier Cooper,[11] who showed that 1176^b 26 ff. is to be taken as distinguishing between a first-class happiness consisting in the exercises of σοφία and an alternative second-class happiness consisting of wisdom and the moral virtues.

Secondly, the argument for saying that understanding is superior to wisdom and the life of the virtues is that it makes its practitioner more self-sufficient: he does not need the money or the cohorts which the pursuer of political happiness does. But if, as Cooper now suggests, the theorizer is also the politician, he *will* need all these things and will lack the self-sufficiency canvassed by book 10.

Will the contemplative of book 10 in fact possess the moral virtues? Some commentators have answered yes, and some have answered no; all have been repelled by the idea of the ruthless, treacherous theorizer, whether or not they regard him as Aristotle's own ideal. But what demands, according to Aristotle, does morality really make of the person of contemplative excellence?

Before answering this question, let us note that there is a distinction, in Aristotle, between failing to possess the moral virtues and falling into moral turpitude. Somebody, without actually being morally virtuous or admirable, may none the less fulfil minimum moral demands such as refraining from murder, theft, and adultery. An Aristotelian moral candidate may, as it were, obtain a pass degree in morality without obtaining the honours degree awarded for the excellence of moral virtue.

The Nicomachean position surely is that the contemplative will *possess* the moral virtues, but that they will not constitute part of his happiness. That will be constituted by contemplation alone. None the less, as a human being, and a good human being, he will practise the moral virtues also. But the activity of moral virtue is given its definition by the mean, and the mean differs from person to person. The right number, for instance, of brave actions will be greater for the politician than it will be for the theorizer. Wisdom, which determines the mean, will prescribe differently in the two cases, because of the different overarching end which

[11] *Reason and Human Good in Aristotle*, 157–60.

constitutes the chief happiness of each of the two types of virtuous person. It will diminish the demands of the other fine and noble activities, in order to preserve the maximum room for contemplative happiness.

Is it not a difficulty that on this view it will not be true that the contemplative does everything else for the sake of contemplation? And if he does not do everything else for the sake of contemplation, how can contemplation constitute his happiness? If he really did everything else for the sake of contemplation, why *should* he rescue his neighbour from burning if it distracts from contemplation?

The difficulty can only be resolved by taking a minimalist interpretation of those passages in the first book of the *NE* which say that happiness is that for the sake of which everything else is done. On the account just given, the contemplative will sometimes do temperate things for the sake of his philosophy (to avoid the hangover which would impede his research, for instance), but he will also do temperate things for their own sake (he doesn't want to let himself get soft, for instance).

The objection to the theorizer, on this interpretation, is not that he will let his neighbour's house burn down, or that he will steal in order to get an adequate research fund. It is rather that he will not do such things as volunteering to fight in the course of a just war. He is likely to take a course of action such as that taken by W. H. Auden at the beginning of the Second World War, staying across the Atlantic to nurture his talent in less dangerous surroundings.

It is noticeable how in the course of the last two decades the positions of the intellectualist interpreters and the comprehensive interpreters of the *NE* have come closer and closer together. But no explanation succeeds in the three goals which most commentators have set themselves: (1) to give an interpretation of book I and book 10 which does justice to the texts severally; (2) to make the two books consistent with each other; (3) to make the resulting interpretation one which can be found morally acceptable by contemporary philosophers. And even if *NE* I and *NE* 10 are reconcilable, the *NE* as a whole seems to have two different heroes: the contemplative of 1 and 10, and the great-souled man of 2–4. Both characters are difficult to make palatable for twentieth-century readers.

But must we judge Aristotle's ethics solely by the Nicomachean position? Those who are prepared to take seriously the *EE* as an expression of Aristotle's mature theory are able to preserve their admiration intact without doing violence to any of the relevant texts of the *NE*. The perfect virtue whose exercise in a perfect life constitutes happiness, according to *EE* 1, is the sum total of the virtues discussed in the central books of the *EE*, and is treated again as a unified whole in the first part of the final chapter of *EE* 8 under the description καλοκἀγαθία.

Clearly, anyone who deserves the description καλὸς κἀγαθός must have all the individual virtues, just as a body can only be healthy if all, or at least the main parts of it, are healthy. Aristotle develops the theme that natural goods, like health and wealth, are beneficial only to a good man; to a bad man they may be positively harmful. But among good men we must distinguish between those of a utilitarian cast, who pursue virtue for the sake of non-moral goods, and the καλοὶ κἀγαθοί who pursue the natural goods only for the sake of the virtuous actions for which they are useful.

For the ideally virtuous man, according to the *EE*, the concepts *good, pleasant*, and *fine* coincide in their application. If what is pleasant for a man differs from what is good for him, then he is not yet perfectly good but incontinent; if what is good for him does not coincide with what is fine for him, then he is not yet καλὸς κἀγαθός but only ἀγαθός; for the καλὸς κἀγαθός the natural goods of health and wealth and power are not only beneficial but fine, since they subserve his virtuous activity. So for him, goodness, fineness, and pleasantness coincide. The bringing about of this coincidence is the task of ethics. But whereas something can be fine or good whether it is a state or an activity, it is only an exercise or activity that can be pleasant. So it is in the fine activities of the good man that the highest pleasure is to be found, and where pleasure, goodness, and fineness meet. But the fine activities of the good man are the exercises of perfect virtue with which happiness was identified in book 1.

Among these are the activities of the philosophic life. If καλοκἀγαθία is a synthesis of the virtues of the parts of the soul in the way that health is a synthesis of the health of various parts of the body, then it must include the virtues of the intellectual parts of the soul as well as of the passional part. But not only is it part of happiness, it also sets the standard to which the activities of the other virtues must conform if they are to remain within the realm of virtue and happiness.

Virtuous action consists in executing choices about the right amount of things – of the passions and external goods which are the field of operation of the moral virtues. What particular behaviour in concrete circumstances counts as virtuous living cannot be settled without consideration of the contemplation and service of God.

In the *EE* Aristotle makes a distinction between constituents and necessary conditions of happiness (1214^b 24–7). Using this terminology, one can bring out clearly the distinction between the two *Ethics*. Whereas in both external goods are only necessary conditions, in the *EE* wisdom plus moral virtue is a constituent of the primary happiness, while in the *NE* it is at best a necessary condition of it. In the *EE* the best of what can be achieved by action is a state in which all the parts of the soul, *qua* human, are operating well. That wisdom plus moral virtue is part of happiness, because of being the right functioning of one part of the soul, is stated most clearly not in an exclusively Eudemian book, but in the common book on the intellectual virtues; but elsewhere I have presented arguments, which I regard as decisive, for showing that this properly belongs with the *EE*. The final book of the *EE* spells out the way in which this happens. The activity of wisdom plus moral virtues is itself part of the exercise of virtue which constitutes happiness; it has an efficient causal relationship to the contemplative happiness, but it is also itself a form of happiness, by being a form of service to God. It contributes to happiness by being part of it, in the way that good breathing contributes to good singing; not in the way that (say) eating certain foods rather than others may contribute to good singing.

'As in the universe, so in the soul, God moves everything by mind', says Aristotle in the final book of the *EE* (1248^a 26). Since the prime mover in the cosmos moves as an object of love, we are left to conclude that the intellectual love of God is, for the *EE*, also the prime motive within the soul. The measure of virtuous living is, for the *EE*, the contemplation and service of God. The old Catholic Catechism, having asked 'Who made you?' and received the answer 'God made me', went on to ask 'Why did God make you?' and answered 'God made me to know him, love him, and

serve him in this life, and be happy with him for ever in the next.'
The account which the *EE* gives of the point of life seems, when
decoded, to be remarkably similar: the key to virtue is to know,
love, and serve God; and that knowledge, love, and service constitute happiness in life, whether it be mortal or immortal.

3

Aquinas on Aristotelian Happiness

Aristotle's treatment of happiness in books 1 and 10 of the *Nicomachean Ethics* has been in recent decades the subject of intense discussion by philosophers. It is perhaps surprising that contemporary writers should find so much to say about chapters that are in themselves tolerably clear and that have been carefully studied for centuries. Some recent readings of the texts are so perverse that they can only be explained by the desire to bring Aristotle's thought into line with contemporary fashion. It provides a useful antidote to any such temptation to play close attention to the Aristotle commentaries of medieval writers who had preoccupations very different from our own.[1]

Accordingly, in this paper I shall consider the treatment of these Nicomachean chapters by St Thomas Aquinas. Just as modern writers strive to make Aristotle relevant to contemporary secular moral concerns, so Aquinas is anxious to enrol the Philosopher in the service of Christian theology. None the less, I shall argue, he has more respect than many of his modern counterparts have for the plain meaning of the texts. The actual use to which the texts are put varies considerably from context to context. I shall consider four different approaches which Aquinas adopts, depending on whether—to put it very crudely—he is at any given moment writing as an Aristotelian, a Christian, a Catholic, or a Dominican.

I

In his commentary on the *Nicomachean Ethics* Aquinas writes as an Aristotelian in the sense that his primary aim is to present the

---

[1] The contemporary discussions are summarized in my book *Aristotle on the Perfect Life* (Oxford, 1992), where also I justify the interpretations of the Aristotelian texts assumed in this essay. All English translations in this essay are mine.

teaching of Aristotle rather than to set forth his own opinion on the matters under discussion. From time to time he draws attention to places where, from a Christian point of view, Aristotle falls short of the truth, but overwhelmingly his concern is with exposition rather than criticism. Though he knows Aristotle only in Latin translation, his commentary is in general remarkably clear and accurate. On the topic of happiness in particular he often grasps Aristotle's meaning where twentieth-century commentators have missed it.

It is common ground among commentators on the *Nicomachean Ethics* (*NE*) that happiness is there defined as the exercise of virtue. Modern interpreters do not agree, however, whether to take it as the exercise of a single dominant virtue, or as the inclusive exercise of all the virtues of the rational soul. Probably a majority of writers in English at the present time favour the inclusive interpretation. When Aristotle says (*NE* 1. 1098ᵃ 17–18) that the good for man is 'activity of soul in accordance with virtue, and if there are several virtues, in accordance with the best and most perfect' these commentators understand 'the best and most perfect virtue' to be the totality of virtues, moral and intellectual.

Aquinas will have none of this. The human good, i.e. happiness, is activity in accordance with virtue, such that 'if there is only one human virtue, the activity which is in accordance with that will be happiness; but if there are several human virtues, happiness will be the activity which is in accordance with the best one of them'.[2] It will turn out, in book 10 of the *NE*, that the best of the human virtues is σοφία or understanding,[3] and that perfect happiness is the exercise of this virtue, namely, the activity of contemplation. But neither Aristotle nor Aquinas explicitly makes this identification in the context of book 1; because at this point no distinction has been made between moral and intellectual virtues,

---

[2] Sequitur quod humanum bonum, scilicet felicitas, sit operatio secundum virtutem: ita scilicet quod si est una tantum virtus hominis, operatio quae est secundum illam virtutem erit felicitas. Si autem sunt plures virtutes hominis, erit felicitas operatio quae est secundum illarum optimam. *In NE* 1.11 [128] (I quote from the Marietti edn.).

[3] The Greek word is often translated 'wisdom'; but this is an inappropriate word in modern English to describe the excellence of the speculative intellect, whereas it corresponds very well to the Greek word φρόνησις which denotes the excellence of the practical reason.

nor, among intellectual virtues, between wisdom (φρόνησις) and understanding.

In *NE* 1 Aristotle gives it as a characteristic of happiness that it should be τέλειον. The Greek word can be rendered into English as 'perfect' or 'complete'. Those who hold an inclusive interpretation of the notion of happiness naturally favour the translation 'complete'. The Latin text which Aquinas used had the translation 'perfectum', and Aquinas takes the key to the meaning of this to be given by Aristotle's explanation at 1097^a 30–^{b}6 of what it is for one good to be more perfect than another.

Some things, Aquinas says in commenting on this text, are desirable only because they are useful; his example is nauseous medicine. There are other things which are both desirable for their own sake and also for the sake of something else. His example here is 'warm and tasty medicine': hot whisky toddy, perhaps, taken to ward off a cold. The second kind of good, he says, is more perfect than the first. The most perfect good is one which is desired only for its own sake and never for the sake of anything else.

Following Aristotle, Aquinas says that an end such as wealth, which is always chosen for the sake of something else, is imperfect, and therefore cannot be identified with happiness: 'The best end, which is the ultimate end, must be perfect. If then there is one such end, this must be the ultimate end we are looking for. But if there are many perfect ends, then it is the most perfect of these which is the best and ultimate.'[4] If 'perfect' were equivalent to 'complete' it would, of course, make no sense to suggest that there could be more than one perfect end. Aquinas takes Aristotle to be saying that there are several perfect ends: honour, pleasure, intelligence, and virtue. But these are not the most perfect, since they are chosen not only for their own sake, but also for the sake of happiness. (Some people, for instance, seek their happiness in pleasure.) Happiness itself is the most perfect, because it alone is chosen only for its own sake and never for anything else.

Aristotle gives self-sufficiency as another characteristic of happiness (1097^{b}14–15). This too has been taken to indicate that

---

[4] Optimus autem finis, qui est ultimus, oportet quod sit perfectus. Unde si unum solum sit tale, oportet hoc esse ultimum finem quem quaerimus. Si autem sint multi perfecti fines, oportet quod perfectissimus horum sit optimus et ultimus. *In NE* 1. 9 [110].

happiness must include many other goods in addition to the exercise of contemplation. Aristotle says 'We think [happiness] most choice-worthy of all things, without being counted along with other things—but if so counted clearly made more choice-worthy by the addition of even the least of goods' (1097^{b}16–20). Supporters of the inclusive notion of happiness have to take the 'if so counted' as a counterfactual whose actualization would lead to an absurdity; they regard the words as meaning 'if it were—*per impossibile*—so counted'.

Aquinas interprets the text quite differently.

The happiness about which he is now talking is self-sufficient because it contains in itself everything which is necessary, but not everything which could come to someone. So it can become better with any other addition. This does not mean that the person's desire remains unsatisfied, since desire regulated by reason, such as the happy person's must be, is not troubled about things which are unnecessary, even if they can be acquired.[5]

This by itself does not, of course, rule out the possibility of happiness containing more than just contemplation; but it does rule out the idea—championed by some of the more extreme critics of the interpretation of happiness as a dominant good— that happiness is a good which is inclusive of all goods.

The seventh chapter of book 10 of the *NE* takes up the discussion of happiness where book 1 left it off. As Aquinas puts it, Aristotle, having shown in the first book that happiness was the exercise of virtue, now goes on to show which virtue it is the exercise of. The best human virtue is the virtue of the best part of a human being, and that is the speculative intellect; hence, it is the activity of the speculative intellect in accordance with its own proper virtue which constitutes perfect happiness.

It is difficult for any commentator to deny that in NE 10 Aristotle makes a very close link between perfect happiness and the exercise of the intellectual virtue of σοφία. Those who favour an inclusive notion of happiness can point, however, to one passage

---

[5] Et sic felicitas de qua nunc loquitur habet de se sufficientiam, qua in se continet omne illud quod est in se necessarium, non autem omne illud quod potest homini advenire. Unde potest melior fieri aliquo alio addito. Non tamen remanet desiderium hominis inquietum, quia desiderium ratione regulatum, quale oportet esse felicis, non habet inquietudinem de his quae non sunt necessaria, licet sint possibilia adipisci. *In NE* 1.9 [116].

which might be taken in their support. Aristotle at 1178^{a}6, having summed up his teaching on perfect happiness by saying that the life of the intellect is the best and pleasantest and happiest life for humans, since a human being is above all else an intellect, then goes on to say, at the beginning of chapter 8, 'And secondly, the one in accordance with the other virtue; for activities in accordance with it are human too. For we display justice and courage and the other virtues in our dealings with one another.' The meaning of 'the one' here is not totally clear, and it is, perhaps, just possible to read the passage as meaning that whereas the principal component of perfect happiness is the activity of the intellect, a secondary component of perfect happiness is the exercise of the moral virtues. But it is more natural to take it as saying either that the life of the moral virtues is a secondary kind of happiness; or, what comes to the same thing, that the person who devotes his life to the display of moral virtue is happy in a secondary sense.

It is thus that Aquinas understands the passage in his commentary. He sums up the message of chapter 8 thus: 'The person devoted to the contemplation of truth is the happiest of all; but happy in a secondary manner is the person who lives in accordance with the other virtue, namely wisdom, which is the guide of all the moral virtues.'[6]

In all the passages which we have considered in detail Aquinas's interpretation is preferable, it seems to me, to the alternative interpretations which have been canvassed by modern commentators. It is not that the idea of happiness as the exercise of all the virtues is not to be found in Aristotle: it is, but in the *Eudemian*, not in the *Nicomachean Ethics*. Aquinas is correct in taking the Nicomachean view to be that perfect happiness consists in theoretical contemplation, and in it alone.

II

As a Christian, Aquinas was anxious to reconcile Aristotle's theory of happiness with the teaching of the Bible and the Church.

---

[6] Cum ille qui vacat speculationi veritatis sit felicissimus, secundario est felix ille qui vivit secundum aliam virtutem, scilicet secundum prudentiam, quae dirigit omnes morales virtutes. *In ME* 10. 12 [2111].

The most authoritative Christian statement on the topic of happiness is of course the set of beatitudes recorded in St Matthew's Gospel as part of the Sermon on the Mount.

Blessed are the poor in spirit: for theirs is the kingdom of heaven.
Blessed are they that mourn: for they shall be comforted.
Blessed are the meek: for they shall inherit the earth.
Blessed are they which do hunger and thirst after righteousness: for they shall be filled.
Blessed are the merciful: for they shall obtain mercy.
Blessed are the pure in heart: for they shall see God.
Blessed are the peacemakers; for they shall be called the children of God.
Blessed are they which are persecuted for righteousness' sake: for theirs is the kingdom of heaven.

St Matthew's Greek word here translated 'blessed' is μακάριος; it is one of Aristotle's words for the happy person, which he often (though not always) uses interchangeably with his more usual word εὐδαίμων. Aquinas uses the Latin word *felix* as the equivalent of εὐδαιμονία, and *felicitas* as the equivalent of εὐδαιμονία when discussing Aristotle; when discussing happiness on his own account, he commonly uses the word *beatitudo*, which he seems to treat as synonymous. It is the word *beatus*, of course, which occurs in the beatitudes, and which relates their content to the Aristotelian discussion of happiness.

It is instructive to read St Thomas's discussion of the beatitudes in question 69 of the *Prima Secundae*. He offers to reveal their structure by reference to the third chapter of *NE* 1 where Aristotle lists three opinions about happiness. Some people, Aristotle there says, identify it with the life of pleasure, others with the active life, and others with the contemplative life. Taking his cue from this passage, Aquinas tells us that the life of pleasure is an impediment to true happiness; the active life is a preparation for it; and the contemplative life is what it essentially consists in.

The first three beatitudes, Aquinas says, show that happiness demands the rejection of the life of pleasure: the poor in spirit reject riches and honours; the meek suppress the passions of anger; those who mourn are those who abstain from the satisfaction of concupiscence. The next two beatitudes are concerned with the active life: those who hunger and thirst after righteousness are those with a passion to carry out their duties to their neighbour; those who are merciful are those who in service to others go beyond the calls of duty and kinship, and consider only the needs of their fellows.

Finally, the remaining beatitudes express the happiness of the contemplative life: the sixth speaks of the vision of God which is promised to the pure in heart, and the seventh is explained thus: 'To make peace in oneself or among others shows that a person is an imitator of God who is the God of unity and peace, and so its reward is the glory of divine sonship.'[7] This sonship is identified by Aquinas with the perfect union with God which is brought about by the supreme contemplative virtue.

The endeavour to bring together the evangelical and the Nicomachean texts can hardly be regarded as successful. Of the first three beatitudes, only the first can plausibly be represented as describing the renunciation of the life of pleasure; it is fanciful to take the word 'mourn' to refer to the suppression of concupiscence, and the control of anger and the pursuit of honour are elements of the second life, the life of action. The fourth and fifth beatitudes fare better: love of righteousness and mercy (or at least equity) are no doubt attributes of any worthy pursuer of the Aristotelian active life, and purity of heart, at any rate in the *Eudemian Ethics*, is a condition of the contemplation of God. But with the seventh and eighth beautitudes the thread is again lost. Peacemaking belongs to the active, not the contemplative, life; and when it comes to the suffering of persecution, St Thomas himself gives up the attempt to match the two systems. What is remarkable about this rapprochement is not that it is done successfully, but that it is done at all. Moreover, it is noteworthy that the Christian texts are distorted to fit the Aristotelian context, rather than the other way round.

III

Aquinas, as a Catholic, had to reconcile Aristotle not only with the biblical texts but with the developed doctrines of the Church. By the time he wrote it was accepted doctrine that the ultimate goal

---

[7] Constituere vero pacem vel in seipso vel inter alios, manifestat hominem esse Dei imitatorem, qui est Deus unitatis et pacis. Et ideo pro praemio redditur ei gloria divinae filiationis, quae est in perfecta coniunctione ad Deum per sapientiam consummatam. *ST* Ia IIae 69. 4c.

of human beings was to be happy, after the ending of this life, in everlasting union with God. It is unclear how far Aristotle believed, when he wrote the *Nicomachean Ethics*, that any part of a human being could survive death—just as (as Aquinas admits) it is unclear how far the happiness described in the beatitudes belongs to the present life and how far it belongs to some other dispensation. It is in the *Secunda Secundae* that we see Aquinas relating the Nicomachean texts to the Christian doctrine of the everlasting happiness of the blessed in heaven.

The second question of the *Prima Secundae* asks where happiness is to be found. Like Aristotle, and often for the same reasons as Aristotle, Aquinas begins by rejecting inadequate popular answers. Happiness is not to be found in riches, or in honours, or in fame, or in power; because all these are exterior things, dependent on chance, all can be used well or badly, and none are self-sufficient. Nor can we find happiness in any of the goods of the human body, such as health and strength. Since all goods are either external goods, or bodily goods, or goods of the soul, shall we then say that happiness is to be found among the goods of the soul? When Aristotle put this question to himself he gave an affirmative answer: happiness is a good activity of the soul (1098^b 13–20). But Aquinas answers by making a distinction. No finite or created good, whether of soul or body, can be the ultimate end which perfectly satisfies our desire.

> But if by the ultimate end we mean the acquisition, or possession, or some kind of use of the thing which is desired as an end, in that case something human within the soul belongs to our ultimate end; because it is by the soul that a human being achieves happiness. The thing which is desired as an end is where happiness is to be found, and what makes one happy; but the acquisition of this thing is what is called happiness.[8]

It is only in God, therefore, that happiness is to be found. But it remains to be explained in what precise relationship to God happiness consists. This is the topic of the eight articles of question 3. Once again, Aquinas takes as his text Aristotle's dictum

---

[8] Sed si loquamur de ultimo fine hominis quantum ad ipsam adeptionem vel possessionem, seu quemcumque usum ipsius rei quae appetitur ut finis, sic ad ultimum finem pertinet aliquid hominis ex parte animae; quia homo per animam beatitudinem consequitur. Res ergo ipsa quae appetitur ut finis, est id in quo beatitudo consistit, et quod beatum facit: sed huius rei adeptio vocatur beatitudo. *ST* Ia IIae 2. 7.

that happiness is activity in accord with perfect virtue (Ia IIae 3. 2, sed contra). It is an activity not of our senses, but of our intellectual part (art. 3) and within the intellectual part it is an activity of the intellect not of the will (art. 4) The enjoyment of the activity is no doubt an activity of the will, but the enjoyment is subsequent to, but not constitutive of, the activity in which happiness consists (q. 2, art. 6; q. 3, art. 4). That activity is an activity of the intellect, and of the speculative rather than the practical intellect (q. 3, art. 5).

Up to this point, Aquinas is in entire accord with the *NE*, and indeed the arguments which he uses to establish that happiness is an activity of the speculative intellect are all drawn from *NE* 10.

If human happiness is an activity, it must be the best human activity. But the best human activity is the activity of the best faculty in respect of the best object. But the best faculty is the intellect, and its best object is divine goodness, which is the object not of the practical but of the speculative intellect. Therefore it is in that activity, namely the contemplation of divine things, in which happiness principally consists . . . [cf. 1177^a 12–21]

Second, the same conclusion is drawn from the fact that contemplation is especially sought for its own sake. The activity of the practical intellect is sought not for itself but for the sake of action, and actions themselves are ordered to some end. Therefore it is clear that the ultimate end cannot be found in the active life, which belongs to the practical intellect. [cf. 1177^b 1–4]

Third, the same conclusion is drawn from the fact that the contemplative life is something a human being shares with superhuman beings, namely God and angels, to which happiness assimilates. But the things which belong to the active life are things in which other animals share, though imperfectly [cf. 1178^b 20–25].[9]

---

[9] Si beatitudo hominis est operatio, oportet quod sit optima operatio hominis. Optima autem operatio hominis est quae est optimae potentiae respectu optimi obiecti. Optima autem potentia est intellectus, cuius optimum obiectum est bonum divinum, quod quidem non est obiectum practici intellectus, sed speculativi. Unde in tali operatione, scilicet in contemplatione divinorum, maxime consistit beatitudo . . .

Secundo apparet idem ex hoc quod contemplatio maxime quaeritur propter seipsam. Actus autem intellectus practici non quaeritur propter seipsum, sed propter actionem. Ipsae etiam actiones ordinantur ad aliquem finem. Unde manifestum est quod ultimus finis non potest consistere in vita activa, quae pertinet ad intellectum practicum.

Tertio idem apparet ex hoc quod in vita contemplativa homo communicat cum superioribus, scilicet cum Deo et angelis, quibus per beatitudinem assimilatur. Sed in his quae pertinent ad vitam activam, etiam alia animalia cum homine aliqualiter communicant, licet imperfecte. Ia IIae 3. 5.

At this point Aquinas seeks to improve on Aristotle, by making a distinction between the perfect happiness to be enjoyed in a future life, which consists in contemplation alone, and the imperfect happiness which is all that we can hope for in the present life. It is only imperfect happiness, he says, which is the topic of Aristotle's book 10 (Ia IIae 3. 6, ad 1). 'The imperfect happiness which can be had in this life consists primarily and principally in contemplation; but secondarily in the operation of practical reason directing human actions and passions as is said in the tenth book of the ethics.'[10] In this passage, unlike the corresponding passage in his commentary, Aquinas seems to side with those who see in *NE* 10 a comprehensive happiness which includes the activity of both speculative and practical intellect.

In the following article, article 6, Aquinas again distances himself from Aristotle, saying that perfect happiness cannot consist in the contemplation of the speculative sciences listed in the *NE*. These sciences, being based on empirical principles, cannot lead beyond the realm of the senses; but the objects of the senses are inferior to human beings. The ultimate perfection of human beings must consist in something which is above the human intellect, and ultimately in the vision of the divine essence (q. 3, art. 6 and 8). The object of the intellect is truth; only God is truth by his own essence, and only the contemplation of God makes the intellect perfect and its possessor perfectly happy (q. 3, art. 7).

Aquinas does not claim the authority of Aristotle for the link which he makes between the Nicomachean theory of contemplative happiness and the Christian doctrine of the beatific vision. But it is not an illegitimate development of Aristotelian theory. Aquinas says, candidly, that the account of happiness given by Aristotle in the *Ethics* concerns a happiness obtainable in the present, everyday, world. But he also draws attention to hints in book 10 that happiness is something superhuman, and that the intellect in which happiness primarily resides is something whose activity is separable from the body. He links these hints to the teaching of the *De Anima* about the independence of the active intellect (1178^a22; *In NE* 10. 12 [2116]).

---

[10] beatitudo autem imperfecta, qualis hic haberi potest, primo quidem et principaliter consistit in contemplatione: secundario vero in operatione practici intellectus ordinantis actiones et passiones humanas, ut dicitur in X Ethic. Ia IIae 3. 5c.

The distinction which Aquinas draws between the imperfect happiness of the present life and the perfect happiness of the divine vision corresponds to an ambiguity in *NE* 10 itself. At one moment Aristotle will say that perfect human happiness consists in contemplation because that is the best activity of the most human thing in us (1178^{a}6). At another time he will say that the life of contemplation is something superhuman (1177^{a}26). He encourages us to 'immortalize as much as possible', identifying ourselves not with our complex human nature, but with its intellectual element. His clinching argument for identifying perfect happiness with contemplation is that this, of all human activities, is the one which is most akin to the activity of God (1178^{b}21–3).

Readers of Aristotle may feel that there is an inconsistency between saying that the intellect is what is most human in us, and also saying that it is superhuman and divine. Aquinas's treatment of happiness in the *Prima Secundae* may be seen as an attempt to resolve this problem. A full understanding of human nature shows, he maintains, that humans' deepest needs and aspirations cannot be satisfied in the human activities—even the speculative activities—that are natural for a rational animal. Human beings can only be perfectly happy if they can share the superhuman activities of the divine, and for that they need the supernatural assistance of divine grace.

Thus, in article 5 of question 5 of the *Prima Secundae* he puts the question: Can human beings, by natural means, acquire happiness? He replies:

The imperfect happiness which can be obtained in this life can be acquired by human beings by natural means, in the same way as the virtues in whose exercise it consists; but perfect human happiness consists in the vision of the divine essence, and to see God in his essence is above the nature not only of human beings but of all creatures.[11]

But does this not fly in the face of the whole Aristotelian doctrine of nature, and of natural teleology? Aquinas puts the objection to himself: 'Nature does not fail to provide what is necessary. But

---

[11] Beatitudo imperfecta quae in hac vita haberi potest, potest ab homine acquiri per sua naturalia, eo modo quo et virtus, in cuius operatione consistit...Sed beatitudo hominis perfecta...consistit in visione divinae essentiae. Videre autem Deum per essentiam est supra naturam non solum hominis, sed etiam omnis creaturae. *ST* Ia, IIae S. 5.

nothing is more necessary for human beings than the means of reaching their final end.' (Ia IIae 5, 1) After all, nature gives irrational creatures all they need to achieve their ends; why not then to human beings also?

His reply is that nature has provided for the bodily necessities of human beings not by giving them fur and claws but by giving them reason to invent and hands to use artefacts. Similarly, nature has not given humans a natural capacity for supreme happiness, but has instead given them free will by which they can turn to God who alone can make them happy. Humans are better off than animals, even though they need outside assistance to achieve their goal, 'Just as A is in a better state with regard to health than B if A can reach perfect health, but only with the aid of medication, while B is capable only of imperfect health even though he can reach it without medical help.'[12]

To give Aristotelian support to this view Aquinas quotes a passage of the *De Caelo* which is only doubtfully relevant.[13] But his development of the Nicomachean doctrine should not be regarded as a perverse assimilation to Christian dogma. Aristotle would no doubt have been surprised at some of the uses to which Aquinas put his treatise, but he could hardly complain that he was completely distorting its meaning. The tension between nature and supernature is there in chapter 7 of book 10 for all to read.

IV

St Thomas was a Dominican friar, a member of the begging ('mendicant') Order of Preachers. Mendicant orders were still a novelty in the Church, and aroused the suspicion and hostility of many conservative churchmen. Members of older religious orders argued that begging was disgraceful for those who could work with their hands; secular clergy resented mendicant

---

[12] Melius est dispositus ad sanitatem qui potest consequi perfectam sanitatem, licet hoc sit per auxilium medicinae, quam qui solum potest consequi quandam imperfectam sanitatem, sine medicinae auxilio. Ia IIae 5. 5, ad 2.

[13] [W]ith men's bodies one is in good condition without exercise at all, another after a short walk, while another requires running and wrestling and hard training, and there are yet others who however hard they worked themselves could never secure this good, but only some substitute for it. *De Carlo*, 292ª25–7.

preachers trespassing in their parishers. Uncomfortably, the rule of the mendicants seemed to blur the familiar boundaries between the active and contemplative religious orders.

Several times in his life Aquinas became embroiled in controversy with anti-mendicants. In describing and justifying the Dominican ideal he once again makes frequent use of Aristotelian texts from the first and last books of the *Ethics*. In particular, in his treatment of the active and contemplative life towards the end of the *Secunda Secundae*, he addresses questions which still preoccupy Aristotelian exegetes.

When Aristotle speaks of a perfect life, for example, what is meant by 'life'? Is it only the chosen supreme activity of the happy person, or does it also include all other vital activities as well? Aquinas, when he introduces the discussion of the active and contemplative life, notes the possible ambiguity; but he makes clear that in this context 'life' means 'what a person most enjoys and is most devoted to'. The active life, then, is one devoted to external actions, the contemplative is one devoted to the contemplation of truth (Ia IIae 179. 1).

Another question currently debated among commentators is this: does Aristotle's contemplative possess the moral virtues or not? The correct answer seems to be that the moral virtues must indeed be possessed by the contemplative, but do not form part of the contemplative's happiness. This too is the answer given by Aquinas: the moral virtues are necessary for the contemplative, to prevent his contemplation being disrupted by passion or tumult, but they are not an essential part of the contemplative life itself (Ia IIae 180. 2).

When he comes to compare the worth of the two lives, Aquinas draws very heavily on Aristotle. To prove that the contemplative life is better than the active, he produces nine arguments. Eight of these are taken verbatim from *NE* 10, 7: the contemplative life is the activity of the best in us; it is the most continuous activity; it is the pleasantest; it is the most self-sufficient; it is sought for its own sake; it is leisurely; it is godlike; it is most truly human. Each text from the *Ethics* is paired with a biblical or patristic text in which, say, Rachel and Leah, or Mary and Martha, are taken as representatives of the two lives. As in the treatment of the beatitudes, more respect is paid to the literal meaning of the Aristotelian texts than to that of the biblical ones.

While Aquinas sides wholeheartedly with *NE* 10 in valuing the contemplative life above the active life, he shifts perspective in an interesting manner when he comes to treat of the vocations of various religious orders. All religious orders, he says, are instituted for the sake of charity: but charity includes both love of God and love of neighbour. The contemplative orders seek to spend time on God alone (*soli Deo vacare*); the active orders seek to serve the needs of their fellows (IIa IIae, 188ª2). Now which are to be preferred, contemplative or active orders (IIa IIae 188. 6)?

Instead of giving an immediate answer, in line with his general Nicomachean preference for contemplation, Aquinas draws a distinction between two kinds of active life. There is one kind of active life which consists entirely in external actions, such as the giving of alms, or the succour of wayfarers; but there is another kind of active life which consists in teaching and preaching. In these activities the religious person is drawing on the fruits of previous contemplation, passing on to others the truths thus grasped. While the purely contemplative life is to be preferred to the purely active life, the best life of all for a religious is the life which includes teaching and preaching. 'Just as it is better to light up others than to shine alone, it is better to share the fruits of one's contemplation with others than to contemplate in solitude' (IIa IIae, 188. 6)[14] St Thomas does not specify what religious order he has in mind; but his phrase *contemplata aliis tradere* is fit to serve as a motto for the Dominican order.

In this final glorification of the ideals of his own order as superior to either of the Nicomachean lives, Aquinas very properly does not make any appeal to Aristotle. Even here, however, there is an instructive comparison to be drawn between the teachings of the two philosophers.

In the *Nicomachean Ethics* Aristotle presents two ideals of happiness: a first-class happiness consisting in pure contemplation, and a second-class happiness consisting in the exercise of wisdom and the moral virtues. In the *Eudemian Ethics* Aristotle presents a single ideal of a happiness which includes both a contemplative and an active element, and which can be summarized as 'the contemplation and service of God'.

---

[14] Sicut enim maius est illuminare quam lucere solum, ita maius est contemplata aliis tradere quam solu contemplari . . . sic ergo summum gradum in religionibus tenent quae ordinantur ad docendum et praedicandum.

Aquinas, in effect, transposes the Nicomachean first-class happiness into a spiritualized after-life where alone it is really at home. In the present life his own ideal—unknown to himself[15]—is much closer to that of the *Eudemian Ethics*, combining contemplation and action, while seeking to practise 'the service of God' in the particular form of teaching and preaching.[16]

[15] I can find no evidence that Aquinas had any first hand knowledge of the *EE*. He frequently quotes 1248ᵃ20–8 to show that God is the origin of our deliberations; but he seems to have known the text only through its occurrence in the anthology *De Bona Fortuna*.

[16] I am grateful to Scott MacDonald and Eleonore Stump for helpful comments on an earlier version of this essay.

4

The Principle of Double Effect

St Thomas Aquinas, in discussing killing in self-defence, remarks that one and the same action may have two effects, one of them intended, and the other beside the intention. Later Catholic theologians developed from this a doctrine of double effect, stated as follows by John of St Thomas. If an act, not evil in itself, has both good and bad effects, then it may be permissible if (1) the evil effect is not intended; (2) the good effect is not produced by means of the bad; (3) on balance, the good done outweighs the harm.

The doctrine of double effect has been much criticized by utilitarians. At first sight, this is perhaps surprising. The principle's reference to an 'act not evil in itself' makes it appear totally to bypass the concerns of utilitarians. For a Catholic who believes in a natural law, there are various classes of acts evil in themselves; but for a thoroughgoing utilitarian, there is no such thing as an act evil in itself without regard to its consequences. Provided the overall outcome is positive, no act, however heinous on the face of it, is absolutely prohibited.

What has excited the ridicule of utilitarians is the consequence to be drawn from the principle of double effect that the intention with which one acts can be a matter of supreme moral significance.

Where Aquinas made a distinction between what was intentional and what was beside the intention, Bentham made a distinction between direct and oblique intention. An act, he said, might be intentional without its consequences being so: 'thus, you may intend to touch a man without intending to hurt him: and yet, as the consequences turn out, you may chance to hurt him'. A consequence may be either directly intentional ('when the prospect of producing it constituted one of the links in the chain of causes by which the person was determined to act') or obliquely intentional (when the consequence was foreseen as likely, but the prospect of producing it formed no link in the determining chain).

Adopting Bentham's terminology we can say that according to the principle of double effect it may sometimes be permissible obliquely to intend a state of affairs which it would be wrong directly to intend. Thus, Catholic theologians have held that if the uterus of a pregnant woman is diseased then in order to preserve her life it may be permissible to remove it, thus causing the death of the foetus. The same theologians would insist that it would be wicked to remove the uterus in order to cause the death of the foetus. Distinctions of this kind, which are applications of the principle of double effect, are commonly held by utilitarians to be sophistical. For this and other reasons the principle of double effect has been poorly regarded by many influential philosophers in the analytic tradition.

In recent times, the principle of double effect has been the subject of prolonged study by Professor Philippa Foot. In 'The Problem of Abortion and the Doctrine of the Double Effect' (1967) she starts her treatment from a series of moral judgements about particular cases. The driver of a runaway tram is right to steer down a track where one man will be killed rather than an alternative track where five men will be killed. On the other hand, a judge who frames and executes one innocent man in order to save five innocents does wrong. Doctors who withhold a scarce drug from a patient who will otherwise die, in order to save five other patients, are right to do so; but it would be totally wrong for a doctor to kill one person to provide spare parts for grafting onto five others who needed them. People who are faced with a choice between rescuing five victims from torture and rescuing one victim are right to choose to rescue the five; on the other hand, there is something wicked about a man who, in order to save five victims from torture, is ready to torture a sixth himself.

The moral difference between the members of these pairs, Foot said, has often been explained by the principle of double effect: that sometimes it is allowable obliquely to intend what one may not directly intend. But this principle leads also to the conclusion that one may not kill an unborn child to save the life of its mother even when both will die in any case; and this, she argued, is intolerable. The difference, therefore, between the members of the pairs is to be explained in terms of the distinction between positive and negative duties rather than in terms of the distinction between direct and oblique intention. We have a much stronger duty to avoid injury than we have to bring aid. The tramdriver faces a conflict of negative duties, the doctors with the scarce drug and the rescuers of the torture victims face a conflict of positive duties. But in each of the cases regarded as immoral the duty to avoid injuring is being sacrificed to the duty to bring aid.

In all these cases, Foot observed, the same moral conclusions could be reached by the use of the positive duty/negative duty distinction as were reached by the use of the direct intention/ oblique intention distinction. In other cases, she claimed, the conclusions will be different, and the advantage seems to be on the side of the positive vs negative principle.

Suppose, for instance, that there are five patients in a hospital whose lives could be saved by the manufacture of a certain gas, but that this inevit-ably releases lethal fumes into the room of another patient whom for some reason we are unable to move. His death, being of no use to us, is clearly a side effect, and not directly intended. Why then is the case different from that of the scarce drug, if the point about that is that we foresaw but did not strictly intend the death of the single patient? Yet surely it is different. (p. 29)

I have no difficulty in accepting Foot's assessment of the vari-ous cases which she takes as the basis of her discussion. Where it is difficult to follow her argument is in its application to the Catholic doctrine that one may not kill an unborn child to save the life of its mother even when both will die in any case. Foot claims that this is an indefensible moral judgement; but it does not appear that the line adopted in her article is sufficient to distinguish her position from the Catholic one at this point.

As we have seen, Foot wished to replace the distinction be-tween direct and indirect intention with the distinction between avoiding an injury and bringing aid. But in the kind of case she has in mind, we are doing an injury to the child in order to bring aid to the mother. The mother will die if we don't kill the child; to bring aid to the mother we do injury to the child. Foot, in this article, deliberately refused to endorse the principle that we may never, whatever the balance of good and evil, bring injury to one for the sake of aid to others, even when this injury amounts to death. But, to judge by the examples on which she based her argument up to this point, she thought that the ratio of the aid given to the harm done must be something more than five to one. It is hard to see, therefore, how she justified killing the child in the case in which mother and child would otherwise both die.

However, in a situation in which nothing that can be done will save the life of child and mother, but where the life of the mother can be saved by killing the child, there is, according to Foot, 'no serious conflict of interests'. I think it is really here that she was looking for the justification of killing in this case. She didn't think, of course, and her whole paper showed this, that a case of this kind is to be settled by working out the interests of the people involved and then choosing that action which will, on balance, serve the greatest interest of the greatest number. For that principle would justify the framing judge and the doctors who kill the patient to produce transplant organs. What, in this context, the reference to the interests of mother and child must mean is that the injury done to the child by killing it is really a negligible injury, since it would soon die anyway.

It is not easy to frame an acceptable principle which would enable Foot to get the conclusion she wanted. It seems too sweeping to say that it is all right to do a certain harm to someone if that harm is going to happen to them anyway. This would mean you could steal anything which was about to be stolen, and rape anyone you saw about to be raped. Of course, it would seem to be reasonable to take something you saw about to be stolen, with a view to returning it later, at a safer time, to its owner. But a principle that you can harm someone to prevent greater harm of the same kind to herself seems to be insufficient to justify the injury done to the child for the sake of the mother. It is difficult to think of a case where one can harm someone to bring aid to someone else, because she is about to suffer that harm anyway, where it would not be justifiable to harm her for this purpose whether or not she was going to suffer the harm anyway.

One case might be where a mountaineer falls and is likely to carry the rest of his rope to their death with him unless the rope is cut between him and the next climber. But the morality of cutting the rope is as hotly debated as the morality of therapeutic abortion. But perhaps this is only because the *certainty* that the others will be killed is unobtainable in the time available for making the decision.

The plea 'If I don't, someone else will' is often used to justify very bad things—e.g. the peddling of dangerous drugs to minors, or the supplying of arms to nations proclaiming their intentions to massacre. At the very least, the principle needed by Foot would have to state, if it is to be tolerable, that the alternative harm which is pleaded as a justification must not be harm produced by human agents. Otherwise, in a sufficiently wicked world, one will be able to justify anything whatever.

In the three cases mentioned by Foot as giving initial plausibility to the principle of double effect, the factor of alternative harm was absent: we were left to assume that the man to be framed would otherwise live in peace, that the corpse to provide the spare parts was a healthy one. In order to know whether Foot had really provided an alternative to the principle of double effect in these cases, we would need to know whether she thought it was all right for the judge to frame a victim, and the doctors to carve up a patient, who was about to die of cancer anyway. Those of us who would shrink from saying this may well wish to defend the importance of the the principle of double effect; and if we wish, like Foot, to dissent from the Catholic view on therapeutic abortion we must do so on other grounds.

By the time she wrote 'Morality, Action and Outcome' (1985) Professor Foot had come to accept the principle which she had attacked in her earlier article. It is not made competely clear what made her change her mind, but in a footnote she explains that a case considered in the 1967 article had left her uncomfortable. In that article she had pointed out that it is possible deliberately to allow something to happen: we might, for instance, think of giving food to a beggar, but then allow him to die so that his body will be available for medical research. Here, she admitted, it did seem morally relevant that in allowing him to die we were aiming at his death. How, without something like the principle of double effect, could she distinguish this from a case where the food was withheld to be given to others in need? Her solution was to suggest that the withholding of food was a violation of negative rather than positive duty. But, as she later came to see, this went far to undermine the positive/negative distinction on which she relied.

In the second article Foot sets out to defend two commonly accepted non-utilitarian principles. The first is that there is a morally relevant distinction between what we do and what we allow to happen. The second is that there is a morally relevant distinction between what we aim at and what we foresee as the result of what we do.

The first of these two principles is akin to the one which, in her earlier article, she wanted to bear the entire weight of supporting the intuitive moral judgements about the particular cases which she considered. The second of the two principles is the principle of double effect which her first article aimed to reject.

To illustrate the first principle, she draws attention once again to the contrast between withholding a scarce medical resource from one patient to save others and killing a patient to bring aid to others. A parallel example is the difference between driving past an injured man in order to bring aid, as fast as possible, to a number of injured people, and driving over a prostrate person for the same purpose.

The difference between doing something and allowing something to happen, Foot says, is not the same as the distinction between act and omission. It is essentially the difference between starting a new train of events, and refusing to intervene to stop one. (There is also the interesting intermediate case of diverting a harmful sequence from one victim to another, as when a pilot whose plane is going to crash steers it from a more to a less inhabited area).

Thus far the argumentation of the second article follows the same lines as the first. But Foot now says that she was wrong, in the earlier article, to say that the distinction between direct and indirect intention was irrelevant to moral judgement. The main part of the second article makes use of the double effect distinction, along with the doing/allowing distinction, in launching an attack on utilitarianism and all forms of consequentialism.

If we are to maintain these two principles, she argues, there is no way in which consequentialism can be amended to make it compatible with them. It will not suffice to modify the utilitarian definition of 'welfare'. Nor is it possible to preserve the principles by adopting a non-utilitarian consequentialism which takes account of rights, and of the violation of rights, in the evaluation of good and bad outcomes.

Some have sought to reconcile the principles with consequentialism by introducing a notion of 'agent-relativity'. But in fact, unless there is some morally relevant difference between my situation and yours, an immoral act done by me is no worse than the same act done by you. 'I do not refuse to kill or torture to prevent others from killing or torturing because I think that killing or torturing is, in the ordinary sense, worse when I do it than when they do.'

To see what is really wrong with utilitarianism, Foot argues, we have to take issue with the whole concept of 'the best state of affairs', the outcome which the utilitarian seeks to bring about. The attraction of utilitarianism is that it can hardly seem rational to prefer a worse to a better state of affairs. But in everyday life a good or a bad state of affairs is one which suits someone's particular interests. The impersonal use of 'good state of affairs' is problematic. Benevolence may be the overarching aim of the utilitarian; but it gives us no reason to say that it would be 'a good state of affairs' or 'a good total outcome' if the sacrificing of a few experimental subjects allowed us to get cancer under control.

Foot's analysis of the motivation of utilitarianism is illuminating, and she is wholly successful in exhibiting the incompatibility between any form of consequentialism and the moral principles from which her article takes its start. But so many philosophers are attracted by one or other form of consequentialism that if told that their theories are incompatible with the principle of double effect their reaction will be not to give up their theories, but to say 'so much the worse for the principle of double effect'.

Given that in her earlier article Foot had herself rejected the principle, one might have expected that in the later one she would have felt obliged to give a full defence of it before using it as a weapon against consequentialism. But at the crucial point of the argument we meet with no more than the following brief passage:

The moral relevance [of the double effect distinction] must be allowed. To be sure it often makes no difference to the injustice of an action whether an injury which it causes is something the agent aims at or something he foresees but has not made the object of his will. A merchant who sold food he knew to be poisonous in order to make money would be morally no better than an unemployed grave digger who deliberately killed to get trade. Nevertheless there are circumstances in which it is morally permissible to bring something about without aiming at it although it would not be morally permissible to aim at it; even though the balance of benefit and harm in the consequences remained the same. That this is so is proved, I think, by some facts about the permissibility of allowing an evil to come on some for the sake of saving others. For sometimes this is a regrettable moral necessity, as in our previous examples having to do with scarce medical resources and with the person lying injured by the roadside. But it does not follow that it would be morally unobjectionable deliberately to leave someone unattended because his death could allow us to save others.

In effect, the only argument used by Foot to show the necessity of the double effect principle (in addition to the distinction between doing and allowing) is the case of the beggar deliberately left to starve, which was mentioned, though not satisfactorily dealt with, in the earlier article. I do not question Foot's judgement that the principle is applicable to this case: but readers of her article may have wondered whether this single case is sufficient to undermine a superstition as widespread as utilitarianism.

In fact, the everyday thinking of ordinary people constantly involves the notion that there can be an important moral difference between aiming at a particular outcome, and bringing about the same outcome without aiming at it. It is easier to see this if we concentrate, initially, on issues which are much less than matters of life and death.

It is an unfriendly act for a hostess deliberately to seat one of her guests at a table next to another guest whom she knows he dislikes. The act is not unfriendly if she assigns the place to the guest not deliberately, but because such is the unintended outcome of a placement which takes account of the conventions about alternating between the sexes, separating husbands from wives, and so on.

In appointing the best candidate to a job, the electors know that they will be causing pain and disappointment to the unsuccessful candidates. This does not make their action wrong. It would be a very different matter to elect a candidate—even if objectively the best candidate—*in order to* cause pain and disappointment to one of the others.

Fixing the date of a board meeting, I may, for good reason, choose one which has the consequence that one of my colleagues cannot attend. That is morally quite different from choosing the same day for the purpose of ensuring that he will be absent.

There are many occasions when, for one reason or another, we have to allow our companions to form a false impression about our intentions or our state of mind. This is quite different from lying, or keeping silent with the purpose of deceiving. My fellow trustees, perhaps, are resolving on an investment in a company which I know, because of confidential information, to be quite unsound. My silence may lead to a disastrous investment; but I am in a very different position from someone who maliciously keeps silent *in order that* his colleagues may invest imprudently.

If we return to the topic of taking life, the necessity for the principle of double effect is in fact brought out by some of the cases which Foot used in the article in which she rejected the principle. Perhaps the clearest is that of the pilot who is steering his stricken plane towards a particular suburb. In one case we may suppose that he is doing this because he wants to minimize the damage caused by his inevitable crash, and the suburb is less populous than any other place he can hope to reach before hitting the ground. In another case we may suppose that he takes the course he does because the suburb is where his wife's lover lives, and he is anxious, when he leaves this life, to take this obnoxious person with him.

There seems to be a big moral difference between these two cases. The difference cannot be explained on utilitarian grounds: the evil outcome is the same in each case. The difference cannot be explained in terms of doing vs. allowing: in each case the pilot kills his victims by crashing his plane upon them; neither is a case of his just allowing them to die. The difference cannot be explained in terms of the distinction between positive and negative duties; in each case the pilot's action conflicts with a negative, not a positive, duty. The crucial difference seems to be that in the one case the death of his victims is merely foreseen as the outcome of his steering away from a more populous area; in the other case the death of at least one of the victims is an end he seeks.

Those who maintain the necessity for the principle of double effect are not committed to maintaining that there will *always* be a moral difference between bringing about an outcome with direct intention and bringing about the same outcome with oblique intention. As Foot says in her second article, a merchant selling food known to be poisonous is no less murderous because his motive is only to make money. But it follows that the case she presented in her first article—of the doctors who produce a healing gas whose manufacture has lethal side-effects on a neighbouring patient—is not by itself any refutation of the doctrine of double effect.

Foot's second article is well inspired, I believe, in turning the tables on the utilitarians with respect to the burden of proof. It is not that the onus is on the double effect principle to defend itself against the presumption that utilitarianism is the only rational moral system. On the contrary, utilitarianism has to defend its abolition of the *prima facie* plausible double effect principle. Anyone who is not an out-and-out act utilitarian will need a double effect principle if she attaches moral importance to the observation of rules or the maintenance of rights. For there will always be cases where the same outcome can be achieved with or without the contravention of a rule or the violation of a right. For the act utilitarian, only the outcome will matter; for others, it will make a difference whether a rule has been contravened or a right violated. And only the principle of double effect enables one to give a consistent articulation of this difference.

Foot sums up the drift of her second article in the following words: 'So far, the argument has tended to resist the encroachment of any form of consequentialism on the "mixed" aim-and-rule morality that we actually seem to have'. To illustrate what is meant by an 'aim-and rule' morality she insists that the aim of benevolence will not justify the killing of the innocent, and that the moral requirement to fight injustice does not imply that one must, or may, fight it by any means whatsoever.

Foot's treatment of the doctrine of double effect does indeed bring out in a vivid manner the essential structure of morality. There are three elements which are essential to a moral system: a moral community; a set of moral values; and a moral code. All three are necessary. First, it is as impossible to have a purely private morality as it is to have a purely private language, and for very similar reasons. Second, the moral life of the community consists in the shared pursuit of non-material values, such as fairness, truth, comradeship, freedom: it is this which distinguishes between morality and economics. Third, this pursuit is carried out within a framework which excludes certain types of behaviour: it is this which marks the distinction between morality and aesthetics.

A common morality, therefore, consists of values and rules. Rules may be absolute, but values are not in the same sense absolute. No value is absolute in the sense that its pursuit justifies the violation of every rule. Some rules are absolute in the sense that their violation is never justified, no matter what the value pursued by their violation. This is simply to say that there are no ends which justify every means, and that there are some means which no end will justify.

Foot's later article discusses in magisterial fashion the relation between values and rules in moral systems. The article does not— apart from references to 'us' and 'the morality we have'—treat explicitly of the nature and extent of the moral community. Moreover, and it may seem surprisingly, the article contains no mention of the issue of abortion which was so central to the 1967 article.

These two omissions are related more than coincidentally. For those who wish to justify abortion do so most effectively when they deny that the unborn are members of the same moral community as adult mothers and surgeons. In this denial, I believe, they are mistaken. But that is a topic for a different essay; for it is the question of membership of the moral community, rather than the principle of double effect, which is the crucial issue when we seek to make a judgement about the morality of abortion.[1]

---

[1] See my 'Abortion and the Taking of Human Life', in *Reason and Religion* (Blackwell, 1987).

II

Philosophy of Mind in the Aristotelian Tradition

5

The Geography of the Mind

In this essay I intend to explore the nature of the mind: to delineate the different mental faculties such as the intellect, the imagination, and the fancy. I shall be, we might say, exploring the geography of the mind: the relations between the senses and the intellect; the contrast between outer senses and inner senses; the two kinds of imagination, fantastic and creative. I shall speak of the intellect as the capacity for operation with signs, and the will as the capacity for the pursuit of rational goals. I shall speak of the relation between the mind, the brain, and the body.

But first, why speak of the mind in these geographic terms at all?

> My mind to me a kingdom is:
>   Such perfect joy therein I find
> That it excels all other bliss
>   That God or Nature hath assigned.
> Though much I want that most would have,
>   Yet still my mind forbids to crave.

So wrote the Elizabethan poet Sir Edward Dyer in a lyric set to music by Byrd four hundred years ago. The theme of Dyer's poem is contentment with one's lot: he seeks of life only a bare sufficiency, aims not at wealth and power:

> ...what I lack my mind supplies
> Lo! thus I triumph like a king,
>   Content with what my mind doth bring.

Other poets besides Dyer have imagined the mind as an inward territory; but not all have seen it as a private kingdom secure from the buffets of the outer world. For Gerard Manley Hopkins it was sometimes a region of terror:

> O the mind, mind has mountains; cliffs of fall
> Frightful, sheer, no-man-fathomed. Hold them cheap
> May who ne'er hung there.
>   (Poem 157, ed. Mackenzie, OUP, 1990)

All of us, at one time or another, are inclined to think of the mind in similar, though less articulate, terms as an inner landscape, whether we look on it with delight like Dyer or with despair like Hopkins. Let us try to evaluate philosophically this metaphor. Let us ask whether, in prosaic truth, there is an inner region within each of us for us to explore; and if so who is the guide who will best help us with the exploration.

It is not easy to give a non-controversial definition of the mind as a starting point for the evaluation of the metaphor of the inner kingdom. Different philosophers would delineate the boundaries of the kingdom in different ways. Historically, there was one conception of mind which dominated philosophical thinking in the centuries when Aristotle was accepted as the doyen of philosophers, and there has been a different one since Descartes inaugurated a philosophical revolution in the seventeenth century.

The old, or Aristotelian, kingdom of the mind had rather narrower boundaries than the new or Cartesian kingdom. For Aristotelians before Descartes the mind was essentially the faculty, or set of faculties, which set off human beings from other animals. Dumb animals and human beings shared certain abilities and activities: dogs, cows, pigs and humans could all see and hear and feel, they all had in common the faculty or faculties of sensation. But only human beings could think abstract thoughts and take rational decisions: they were marked off from the other animals by the possession of intellect and will, and it was these two faculties which essentially constituted the mind. Intellectual activity was in a particular sense immaterial, whereas sensation was impossible without a material body.

For Descartes, and for many others after him, the boundary between mind and matter was set elsewhere. It was consciousness, not intelligence or rationality, that was the defining criterion of the mental. The mind, viewed from the Cartesian standpoint, is the realm of whatever is accessible to introspection. The kingdom of the mind, therefore, included not only human understanding and willing, but also human seeing, hearing, feeling, pain and pleasure. For every form of human sensation, according to Descartes, included an element that was spiritual rather than material, a phenomenal component which was no more than contingently connected with bodily causes, expressions and mechanisms.

Descartes would have agreed with his Aristotelian predecessors that the mind is what distinguishes human beings from other animals. But for them what made this true was that mind was restricted to intellect, and only humans had intellect; for him what made it true was that though mind included sensation, only humans had genuine sensation. Descartes, that is to say, denied that animals had any genuine consciousness. The bodily machinery which accompanies sensation in human beings might occur also in animal bodies; but a phenomenon like pain, in an animal, was a purely mechanical event, unaccompanied by the sensation which is felt by humans in pain.

By introducing consciousness as the defining characteristic of mind, Descartes in effect substituted privacy for rationality as the mark of the mental. The intellectual capacities which distinguish language-using humans from dumb animals are not in themselves marked by any particular privacy. Whether Smith understands quantum physics, or is motivated by political ambition, is something which a third party may be better able to judge than Smith himself. In matters such as the understanding of scientific theory and the pursuit of long-term goals the subject's own sincere statement is not the last possible word.

On the other hand, if I want to know what sensations someone is having, then I have to give his utterances a special status. If I ask him what he seems to see or hear, or what he is imagining or saying to himself, what he says in reply cannot be mistaken. Of course it need not be true—he may be insincere, or misunderstand the words he is using—but it cannot be erroneous. Experiences of this kind have a certain property of indubitability, and it was this property which Descartes took as the essential feature of thought. Such experiences are private to their owners in the sense that while others can doubt them, they cannot.

Privacy of this kind is quite different from the rationality which pre-Cartesians took as the defining characteristic of mind. It is thus that human sensation falls, for Descartes, within the boundaries of the mental, whereas for the pre-Cartesian it fell without.

In addition to intellection and sensation there are other human capacities and activities which philosophers have identified as mental; memory, for instance, and imagination and the passions or emotions. Some philosophers have classified memory and imagination as inner senses: they have regarded these faculties as senses because they saw their function as the production of imagery; they regarded them as inner because their activity, unlike that of the senses, was not controlled by external stimuli.

The theory of inner sense was common to both Aristotelian and Cartesian accounts of the mind. It took, however, different forms within the different traditions. In one interpretation of Aristotle the inner sense of imagination was seen as active not only in the absence of external stimuli, but also whenever the outer senses themselves were active: the operation of the senses, on this interpretation, consisted in triggering off the imagination to produce the appropriate inner image. In the post-Cartesian psychology of Hume, the deliverances of the outer senses are impressions, the deliverances of the inner senses are ideas; the whole content of our minds, the phenomenal base from which the whole of the world is to be constructed, consists of nothing but impressions and ideas.

Most importantly, for the post-Cartesian empiricist tradition which flowers in Hume, the meaning of the words of our language consists in their relation to impressions and ideas. It is the flow of impressions and ideas in our minds which make our utterances not empty sounds, but the expression of thought; and if a word cannot be shown to refer to an impression or to an idea it must be discarded as meaningless.

Though the theory of the inner sense can be found both in medieval Aristotelianism and in post-Cartesian psychology, it took radically different forms in the two traditions. In particular, the relation between imagery and language was conceived quite differently by an Aristotelian such as Aquinas and a British empiricist such as Hume. Aquinas agreed with the empiricists that wherever there was thought there must be a flow of imagery: but for him it was not the images which gave content to the thought, but the thinking activity of the intellect which gave meaning to the images in the imagination.

For reasons which have been presented convincingly in our own time by Wittgenstein, I believe that Aquinas was correct, against the empiricists, in his view that when we think in images it is thought that confers meaning on the images, and not vice versa. We do much of our thinking by talking silently to ourselves; but the procession of imaged words through our imagination would not constitute a thought, would not have the meaning it does, were it not for our mastery of the language to which the words belong, a mastery which is an achievement of our intellectual power, not of our image-making faculty.

We can convince ourselves of this if we reflect on what happens in these cases where our imagination is concerned with symbols such as spoken or written words. If I call to mind the image of an advertisement in an unknown tongue, seen on a hoarding in a foreign city, the presence of that image in my imagination does not mean that I have in my mind the thought the imagined words express. But the point is not restricted to where the images in our minds are images of symbols. When our private thoughts are embodied not in imagined words, but in other visual or aural images, here too, as reflection will show, the image carries no unambiguous meaning on its face. My mental image of Napoleon may or may not resemble Napoleon; but my mental image of Abraham certainly does not, since I have not the faintest idea what Abraham looked like. An image does not get its significance by any resemblance to what it is an image of; to have meaning it must be employed in a particular way by the intellect. In the book of our thoughts, one might say, it is the intellect that is the author who provides the text; the imaging faculty is no more than typesetter and illustrator.

An empiricist philosopher might be willing to accept the claim that images possess the meaning they do only when they are in the mind of a language-user. But she might maintain that the mastery of language is something which is itself to be explained in terms of laws of association between images in succession. Whereas Aquinas, in the Middle Ages, and Chomsky, in our own time, would insist that language acquisition can only be explained if we postulate a species-specific ability in human beings. Domestic animals live in the same sensory environment as human babies, yet seem unable to achieve the mastery of abstract and universal terms which the child acquires as it grows. Aquinas was willing enough to attribute inner senses to animals no less than to humans; but for language-acquisition, he insisted, an inner sense was not enough, an intellect was necessary. In the empiricist account of mind he would have failed to recognize anything which he would call the intellect: the empiricist programme might be described in his terms as the endeavour to eliminate the intellect in favour of the inner sense.

In fact, I believe that the notion of 'inner sense' is misleading, whether in the scholastic or the empiricist tradition. It is not, in my view, the appropriate concept with which to grasp the nature of a faculty such as the imagination. How then are we to characterize the imagination? We must begin by making a distinction.

By 'imagination' there are at least two things which we can mean. We may mean simply the ability to call up mental images; an ability which each of you can exercise now simply by shutting your eyes and imagining what I look like, or by sitting in silence and reciting the Lord's prayer to yourselves. Much work in modern psychology and philosophy has gone to show that the imagination, in this sense, is incapable of performing the explanatory tasks which empiricist psychology attributed to it, and is unamenable to scientific study by introspection. I believe that these contentions of contemporary behaviourism are justified: but it would be foolish to be led by them to deny the very existence of the imagination in the sense of the power to call up images. The imagination, in this sense, is a power that is generally shared by members of the human race.

There is another sense of the word in which imagination is a much less evenly distributed faculty. The ability to imagine the world different in significant ways; the ability to conjecture, hypothesize, invent—this is a second form of imagination, creative imagination. Creative imagination is what poets, storytellers, and scientists of genius have *par excellence*.

Neither of the two kinds of imagination we have distinguished can be identified simply with the human intellect in the sense of the ability to master language. Take first the capacity for imaging, which gives us the ability to talk to ourselves. This is a gift which is minor in comparison with the ability to talk at all: there could be a race just as intelligent as us which could think only aloud, and not in privacy; their lives would be both more honest and more noisy than ours, but there would be nothing in the world which would be beyond their ken without being also beyond ours. But if the imagination, in this first sense, is something inferior to the intellect, the imagination, in the second sense, is something superior to the intellect: it is the ability not just to understand language, but to use language creatively, to form new thoughts and discover new truths and build new worlds.

In tribute to Coleridge, but without claiming fidelity to the criteria by which he makes his distinction between two faculties, I will call the imagination in the first sense the *fancy*, while reserving the word 'imagination' for the creative imagination.

Like Coleridge, too, I shall feel the need to make a further subdivision within the realm of the creative imagination. Such imagination, I have maintained, is exhibited by geniuses both in science and in poetry. Both scientific and poetic imagination involves the mastery of language. Language is used in the framing of hypotheses no less than in the writing of drama. But when Darwin framed the hypothesis of evolution by natural selection, he did not need to use language in any non-literal manner. But it is one of the characteristics of the literary imagination that it is intimately linked with the ability to use language figuratively, in symbolic images, so that the literary imagination is called 'imagination' by a double title.

Not only poets, but prophets and divines have claimed that there is a special link between their calling or craft and its expression in imagery. Sometimes the claim takes the following form. Language in its literal sense is adapted to cope with material objects, with bodily entities. But the poet, the prophet, the divine, are concerned with matters spiritual, not bodily. Therefore they can use language only figuratively. An argument of this form sometimes seems to lurk behind some theological presentations of the theory of the analogical nature of religious discourse.

For present purposes, let us restrict our attention to the more humble faculty of the fancy. It is the imagination in this sense which philosophers have been inclined to call an inner sense. It was a faculty which differed from outer senses like sight in having an organ and an object inside the body (in the brain) rather than an organ at the edge of the body (like an eye) and an object outside the body (like the trees I see).

In fact, the fancy is a faculty quite different from senses such as sight or smell or touch. Sense faculties are faculties for discriminating between public objects which different subjects, depending on their circumstances, may be in better or worse positions to observe. Sense faculties operate by means of organs, that is, parts of the body which can be voluntarily controlled in characteristic ways which affect the efficiency of the discrimination. But the objects of the fancy are created, not discovered; there is no such thing as gradual approximation to their optimal discernment, or control by one observer on another's acuity of discrimination. The eye may be screwed up to see more clearly, or the ear cocked to hear more sharply; but there is no organ which can be deployed to capture an image more vividly. Using one's fancy is not discriminating between images: it is fantasizing discrimination between objects.

The fancy is not, then, a sense. Is it a part of the mind? According to the Aristotelian tradition, no; according to the Cartesian tradition, yes. The answer to the question, if the fancy is not a sense, must depend on its relationship to the intellect. And that cannot be decided until we have offered some attempt to delineate the intellect itself.

The human intellect is the capacity for intellectual abilities. It is a capacity, not an activity: babies have minds even though they do not yet exhibit intellectual activities. It is a second-order capacity: an ability to acquire abilities. To know a language is to have an intellectual ability: the ability to speak, understand, and perhaps read the language. To have an intellect is to have a capacity one stage further back: the ability to acquire abilities such as the knowledge of a language.

Intellectual abilities are abilities for intellectual activities. Intellectual activities are ones which involve the creation and utilization of symbols. Mathematics, philosophy, portrait painting and poetry are clearly intellectual activities by this definition. The definition, you will have observed, has an indistinct borderline; this is a merit of the definition, since the concept it is aimed to capture is a fuzzy concept.

The most important intellectual skill is the mastery of language. Others, such as knowledge of mathematics, are acquired by human beings through the languages they have mastered. So the study of the acquisition and exercise of language is the way *par excellence* to study the nature of the human mind. To study knowledge of language you have to consider what the exercise of linguistic knowledge is. The exercise of linguistic knowledge is linguistic behaviour: but 'behaviour' here must be understood broadly, so that, for instance, reciting a poem to myself in my head imperceptibly to others will count as an instance of linguistic behaviour.

I have delineated the senses, the fancy, and the intellect. Where now are we to place the boundary of the mind? The geography of the mind, it is clear, is not a simple matter to discover. Already we have seen that its most basic features are a matter of dispute between philosophers. It cannot be explored simply by looking within ourselves at an inward landscape laid out to view. What we see when we take this inner look will be partly determined by the philosophical viewpoint from which we look, or, we might say, by the conceptual spectacles we may be wearing.

But at this point I should make my own position clear: I believe that the clearest insight into the nature of the mind is to be obtained from the Aristotelian viewpoint. The mind is to be identified with the intellect, that is, the capacity for acquiring linguistic and symbolic abilities. The will, too, is part of the mind, as the Aristotelian tradition maintained, but that is because intellect and will are two aspects of a single indivisible capacity, as I will shortly go on to explain.

It may be argued that the definition of the mind as an intellectual capacity is too austere and abstract. Some may feel that it is a perverse denial of the reality of the mind. Surely the mind is not just a faculty: it is an immaterial and private world, the locus of our secret thoughts, the auditorium of our interior monologues, the theatre in which our dreams are staged and our plans rehearsed.

Now it would be folly to deny that human beings can keep their thoughts secret, can talk to themselves without making any noise, can sketch figures before their mind's eye instead of on pieces of paper. But the capacity for mental imagery of this kind—visual, audio-motor, and other imagery—has already been described and named: it is not the intellect, but the fancy.

Moreover, the fancy, no less than the intellect, is a capacity or faculty. Particular exercises of the imaginative fancy are psychological events, occurring at particular times and places; they are experiences, in relation to which the subject is in a uniquely authoritative position. (The authority she has, though, is the authority of the judge, not of the witness.) These psychological events occur with great frequency in our lives; they may play a

greater or lesser part in our lives according to the active or contemplative nature of our temperament and vocation.

To understand the nature either of the intellect or the fancy the
philosopher has to reflect on the nature of ability in general.
Abilities are distinct from their exercises: an ability is a more or
less enduring state, the exercise of an ability will be a datable
event or process. Whisky, for instance, even while standing harm-
lessly in the bottle possesses the ability to intoxicate; it only begins
to exercise it after being imbibed.

Abilities must be distinguished not only from their exercises
but also from their possessors and their vehicles.

The possessor of an ability is what *has* the ability: in this case of
human abilities, the human being in question. It is I, and not my
mind, who know English and am exercising this ability in writing
this essay.

The vehicle of an ability is the physical structure in virtue of
which the possessor of an ability possesses the ability and is able
to exercise it. The distinction between abilities and their vehicles
is not something which is peculiar to human beings and their
abilities. The vehicle of the whisky's power to intoxicate is the
alcohol the whisky contains. A vehicle is something concrete,
something which can be weighed and measured; an ability, on
the other hand, has neither length nor breadth nor location. This
does not mean that an ability is something ghostly: my front-door
key's ability to open my front door is not a concrete object, but it is
not a spirit either.

Though the distinctions we have drawn are not restricted in
their application to the abilities of human beings, they have many
applications in the human realm and are vital to our attempt to
delineate mental geography. An important instance of the distinction between possessor, ability, and vehicle is the distinction
between people, their minds, and their brains.

Human beings are living bodies of a certain kind, with various
abilities. The mind, as we have said, is *par excellence* the intellect,
the capacity to acquire or possess intellectual abilities. The vehicle
of the human mind is, very likely, the human brain. Human
beings and their brains are physical objects; their minds are not,
because they are capacities. Once again, to say that the mind is not
a physical object is not to say that it is a ghostly spirit. If I insist
that a mind is not a physical object with a length and breadth and

location, that is not out of devotion to spiritualism, but simply out
of concern for conceptual clarity.

The distinctions which I have been making are not novel: they
are developments of distinctions which go back at least as far as
Aristotle. However, philosophers have been tempted in every age
to blur the distinctions: they like to reduce potentialities to actualities. Some philosophers attempt to reduce powers to their
exercises: thus, explicitly, David Hume, who said the distinction
between a power and its exercise was frivolous. Some philosophers attempt to reduce powers to their vehicles: thus, implicitly, Descartes, who wanted to identify the powers of bodies with
their geometrical properties.

Philosophical errors about capacities in general show up particularly vividly when they occur in the philosophy of mind.
Applied in this area, exercise-reductionism becomes behaviourism: the attempt to identify mind with behaviour consists in
treating the complex second-order capacity which is the mind as
if it was identical with its particular exercises in behaviour.
Applied in this area, vehicle-reductionism becomes materialism:
the attempt to identify mind with brain consists in reducing my
mental capacities to the parts and structures of my body in virtue
of which I possess those capacities.

Materialism is a grosser philosophical error than behaviourism
because the connection between a capacity and its exercise is in
truth a more intimate one than the connection between a capacity
and its vehicle. In the case of the mind, the connection between
capacity and exercise is a conceptual connection: one could not
understand what the mind was if one did not understand what
kinds of thing constitute the exercise of mental capacity. The
connection between capacity and vehicle, on the other hand, is a
contingent one, discoverable by empirical science.

If the mind is not a physical structure how can one talk, even
metaphorically, about the geography of the mind? Can the mind
have a structure at all, if it is not a concrete object? The answer is
yes, provided that we are clear what kind of structure we are
talking about.

The set of abilities through which the mental capacity is exercised have relationships to each other, and these relationships
between abilities form the structure of the mind. There are, for
instance, relationships between the ability to multiply and the

ability to take square roots. Once again, this is not something peculiar to minds, and the structure in question is not a ghostly partitioning. Not only human beings have abilities which are structured in this way: we can discover the structure latent in the operations of a pocket calculator by identifying the algorithms it uses (which we might do, for instance, by identifying the different kinds of rounding errors which occur in its output).

There is a distinction between the structure of the mind, in this sense, and the structure of the brain which is its vehicle. Here again, the analogy with the calculator helps to make the point clear, because there too there are different kinds of structure: it is the mathematician who identifies the structure of the algorithm, the engineer who is the expert on the structure of the electronic hardware.

I have several times denied that the mind is to be identified with the brain. There is a venerable tradition which denies that the intellect has a bodily organ at all: for Aquinas, for instance, the brain was the organ of the fancy, but there was no organ of any kind for the intellect. The thesis which I have been defending needs to be distinguished from Aquinas's theory.

Aquinas does not, as I do, make a systematic distinction between the organ and the vehicle of a faculty. I use the word 'organ' in a way suggested by its etymology and consistent with the use of the word to describe the eye as the organ of sight. In my view, a sense organ is something like a tool, a part of the body which can be voluntarily moved and used in characteristic ways which affect the efficiency of the discriminatory activity which it serves. In this sense there is no organ of the intellect, nor of the fancy either: I cannot move my brain in order to imagine better in the way that I can turn my eyes to see better. Even if brain activity is a necessary condition for thought, this does not make the brain an organ of thought in the way that the eyes are organs of sight and the tongue and palate are organs of taste. But if we distinguish between organ and vehicle, then we can say that the brain is the vehicle both of the fancy and of the intellect.

What, now, is the relation between senses, fancy, and intellect: how are these faculties which we have distinguished interrelated with each other? Let us consider first the relationship in the context of the acquisition of concepts, and then in the context of the exercise of concepts.

In order to possess a concept of something which can be an object of experience, it is not sufficient simply to have the appropriate experience. Young children see coloured objects before they painfully acquire colour-concepts; dumb animals can see and taste a substance such as salt but they cannot acquire the concepts which language-users can exercise in general judgements about salt. A special ability unshared by animals is necessary if human beings are to acquire concepts from the experience which they share with animals.

The mind is not just the ability to acquire abilities such as concepts: it is the ability to exercise them in appropriate conditions. It not only harvests ideas from experience, it gathers them in: it is the storehouse of ideas. Varying the metaphor, the intellect when it commences its activity, is an unwritten tablet, a *tabula rasa*. As concepts and beliefs are acquired by the operation of the specifically human intelligence, the tablet becomes covered with writing, the empty barn fills up. The mind has contents as well as powers. To find out the contents of a person's mind at a given time, you must find out what she understands, what she knows, what she believes at that moment.

The ideas, that is to say the concepts and beliefs, of the intellect are exercised in various ways. Just as the senses are necessary but not sufficient for the acquisition of ideas so, too, sense and fancy are necessary for the exercise of ideas. If there is to be an exercise of concepts, or the application of knowledge, there must be some exercise of sense or fancy, some application to a sensory context.

This necessity obtains whether the concepts are concrete or abstract, whether the truths known are necessary or contingent. For a man to be exercising the concept, say, of red, it seems that he must be either discriminating red from other colours around him, or having a mental image of redness, or a mental echo of the word 'red', or be talking, reading or writing about redness, or something of the kind. He may indeed be able to *possess* the concept *red* without this showing in his experience or behaviour on a given occasion, but it seems that without some embodiment in sensory activity there could be no *exercise* of the concept on that occasion. Similarly, with the knowledge of a general truth, such as that two things that are equal to a third are equal to each other. For this knowledge to be exercised it seems that its possessor must either enunciate it, or apply it say in the measurement of objects, or utilize it in some other way even if only in the artful manipulation of symbols.

Once one has described the intellect and the fancy and grasped their relationship to each other, it does not greatly matter what answer one gives to the question earlier postponed: is the fancy a part of the mind? The Aristotelian tradition which I am defending is perhaps best expressed by saying that in the geography of the mind the homeland is occupied by the intellect. The fancy and the senses are regions which are not part of the mind strictly so called: they are colonies rather than metropolitan areas. They are indeed well colonized: the images which occur in the fancy have the meaning they have because of the intellectual skills of the person whose fancy it is; the senses of a language-user perceive the world structured by the categories of the language of which the intellect is master. But they are not strictly part of the mind.

One question remains which must be addressed before this essay ends. One may ask where, in all this geography of the mind, is the location of the affective side of humanity: the emotions and the will? A full answer to this question would need a whole lecture. The contrast between cognitive and affective, in human life, cuts across the stratification of senses, fancy, intellect. But I promised in this essay to consider the relation between the intellect and the will. Doing so will illustrate what we are about when we regionalize the mind into faculties.

Human beings do many things such as understanding, judging, feeling, desiring, deciding, intending. Philosophers ascribe these different states and activities to different faculties. Why? What is it to ascribe particular actions to one or other faculty? It is to group the actions together in virtue of common features of description and assessment which apply to them.

Among the characterizations we may assign to human mental states and actions, there are two which stand out as the most important. We may characterize certain states as true (or false); we may characterize others as good (or evil). Beliefs, most obviously, may be described as true or false; desires, most obviously, may be described as good or evil. Those states and activities which can be evaluated on the true/false scale belong to the cognitive side of the soul; those states and activities which are evaluated on the good/evil scale belong to the affective, volitional side of the soul. At the highest level, the truth-bearing (or false-ness-bearing) items are actualizations of the intellect; the good-ness-bearing (or badness-bearing) items are actualizations of the will.

States of the will and activities of the intellect may both be described as right or wrong, it is wrong to think that the earth is larger than the sun, and wrong to have vengeful strategies; but the wrongness in the one case consists in falsehood, and in the other case in evil. The right, we might say, is the genus of which the true and the good are the species. Similarly, the human mind is a capacity of which the intellect and the will are the primary faculties.

The intellect and the will can be thought of as two aspects of the ability to master language. We make use of language both to understand the world and to control and alter the world. The intellect is the power to receive and process linguistic input: to understand what we are told by others, to categorize the world we experience in terms of the concepts of our language. The will is what gives the linguistic dimension to our behavioural output: it is the power to pursue the long-term goals which can be formul-ated only in language, and to enrol other language-users, by command and request, in our pursuit of those goals. Intellect and will are therefore two aspects of the overall ability to master and employ language which is the essence of the human mind.

6

Body, Soul, and Intellect in Aquinas

St Thomas Aquinas, who in the twentieth century has been considered an official spokesman for Roman Catholic orthodoxy, was in his own day an adventurous philosopher whose teaching was regarded by many theologians with suspicion. Just three years after his death the congregation of Oxford university, following the lead of colleagues in Paris, condemned, without naming him, a number of propositions which he had maintained. Those who taught these Thomist theses were to be allowed forty days to recant; if they continued to hold them they were to lose their MAs.

The part of Aquinas's teaching which got him into trouble at Oxford was his application of the Aristotelian theory of form and matter to the nature of the human soul. For Aristotle material substances like a bit of wood consisted of matter possessing certain forms. A piece of wood possesses accidental forms, such as its shape, colour, and temperature which can be varied while it remains wood; it also possesses a substantial form which makes it the kind of thing it is, namely wood. If it is burnt and turns into ash so that it ceases to be wood, then the same matter which once existed with the substantial form of wood now exists with the substantial form of ash. The very same parcel of matter was once wood and is now ash. What was it all the time? Nothing, said Aquinas; all that remains in common is identity of matter—prime matter, in the technical expression, namely matter considered in abstraction from any particular form it may take as one or other particular kind of matter.

Following Aristotle, Aquinas used the doctrine of matter and form as the key to the relationship between soul and body. For Aristotle animals and vegetables had souls no less then human beings. The vegetative, or nutritive, soul was the explanatory principle of the growth and propagation of plants; the sensitive soul was the explanatory principle of the sensory activities of animals. What made human beings special was not simply the possession of a soul, but the possession of a rational or intellectual soul. Now human beings grow and take nourishment, just as plants do; they see and taste and run and sleep just as animals do. Does that mean that they have a vegetable and animal soul as well as a human soul?

Many of St Thomas's contemporaries answered in the affirmative. In a human being, they maintained, there was not just a single form, the intellectual soul, but also sensitive and nutritive souls governing the animal and vegetable functions of the human being. Some theorists added, for good measure, a form which made a human being a bodily being, namely a form of corporality, which humans had in common with sticks and stones just as they had sensitive souls in common with animals and vegetative souls in common with plants.

St Thomas rejected the proliferation of substantial forms. In a human being, he maintained, there was only a single substantial form, namely the rational or intellectual soul. It was that soul which controlled the animal and vegetable functions of the body; and there was no need of a substantial form of corporality. If there was a plurality of forms, he argued, then it would not be the same entity, the same person, which both saw and thought. When a human being died there was nothing in common between the living person and his corpse other than the basic prime matter. It was this teaching of St Thomas which was condemned at Oxford in 1277. The doctrine of the plurality of forms was imposed upon the University.

Aquinas's teaching about the intellectual soul is the key to his psychology. The intellect, or intellectual soul, was peculiar to human beings. It was what marked them off from animals. The Latin word *intellectus* is connected with the verb *intelligere*: this is commonly translated 'understand', but in Aquinas's Latin it is a verb of very general use corresponding roughly to our word 'think'.

We employ the word 'think' in two different ways: we talk of thinking *of* something, and we talk of thinking *that* something. Thus, in the first way, we may say that someone abroad thought of home, or thought of his family; in the second way we may say that someone thought that there was a prowler downstairs, or that inflation was on the increase. Aquinas makes a corresponding distinction between simple thoughts (thoughts *of*) and complex thoughts (thoughts *that*); both of these were acts of intellect. All thoughts, according to Aquinas, are expressible in language.

This does not mean that all thoughts are given public expression in words; I may mutter an insult behind clenched teeth, and some thoughts are not put into words even in the privacy of the imagination. The wanderer's thought of his family at breakfast may simply be an image of them sitting in the kitchen, not the internal enunciation of any proposition.

If the intellect is the capacity for thought, how can it be something peculiar to human beings? Surely a dog, seeing his master take the lead off the hook, thinks that he is going to be taken for a walk and expresses the thought quite clearly by leaping about? Aquinas does in fact allow animals the ability to think simple thoughts; but what is special to human beings is the relationship between thought and language. The intellect is best defined as the capacity for thinking those thoughts that only a language-user can think, thoughts for which no expression in non-linguistic behaviour can be conceived (e.g. the thought that truth is beauty or that there are stars many light-years away).

Aquinas believed that all the ideas of the intellect are in some way dependent on sense-experience; but the way in which he believed ideas to be abstracted from experience was a complicated one. The intellect was not one faculty, but two; or rather a single faculty with two powers: the agent intellect and the receptive intellect. It was the agent intellect which was the human capacity to abstract universal ideas from particular sense-experience; it was the receptive intellect which was the storehouse of those ideas once abstracted.

Aquinas postulated an agent intellect because he thought that the material objects of the world we lived in were not, in themselves, fit objects for intellectual understanding. A Platonic idea, universal, intangible, unchanging, unique, existing in a noetic heaven, might well be a suitable object for intellectual understanding; but there are no such things as Platonic ideas. Things in the physical world are in themselves, according to Aquinas, only potentially thinkable or intelligible. An animal with the same senses as ours perceives and deals with the same material objects as we do; but he cannot have intellectual thoughts about them or a scientific understanding of their nature, because he lacks the light cast by the agent intellect. We humans, because we can abstract ideas from the material conditions of the natural world, are able not just to perceive but to think about and understand the world.

Aquinas did not teach that the human intellect can know nothing but its own ideas; but he did believe that it was impossible to grasp material objects by a purely intellectual thought. The reason is that the principle of individuation for material objects is individual matter; and our intellect understands by abstracting ideas from such matter. But what is abstracted from individual matter is universal. So our intellect is not directly capable of knowing anything which is not universal. No matter how full a description I give of an individual, no matter what congeries of properties I ascribe to her, it is always logically possible that more than one individual satisfies the description and possesses the properties. Unless I bring in reference to particular times and places there may be no description I can give which could not in theory be satisfied by a human being other than the one I mean. I cannot individuate the person I mean simply by describing her appearance, her qualities. Only perhaps by pointing, or taking you to see her, or calling to mind an occasion on which we met, can I make clear beyond doubt which person I mean; and pointing and vision and this kind of memory are matters of sense, not of pure intellectual thought.

Intellectual knowledge of the individual, for Aquinas, must always be through cooperation between the intellect and the senses, by the joint use of our intellectual and sensory faculties, including imagination and memory. It is only by linking intellectual ideas with sensory experience that we know individuals and are capable of forming singular propositions such as 'Socrates is a man'. Aquinas called this relationship of the intellect to the sensory context of its activity 'Reflection upon phantasms'.

What are phantasms? From the role assigned to them in Aquinas's account of knowledge of individuals, it looks as if the notion of phantasm covers the whole of sense-experience: actual perception no less than imagination. Sometimes St Thomas writes as if he believed that whenever I am doing a bit of real seeing— e.g. looking at a beetle crawling across my desk—there is taking place, simultaneously, in my imagination, a replicating play of mental images representing a beetle crawling across my desk. If he really held this, I think he was wrong; but not in a way which damages his general account of knowledge of the individual.

Sometimes, too, he writes as if when we think of things in their absence, we do so by means of mental images of them; so that I think of the Statue of Liberty by picturing the Statue of Liberty. But there are a number of places where he qualifies this. He does indeed believe—and I think rightly—that we cannot think of things in their absence without using mental images: there has to be *something* going on in our imagination if we are to have a datable thought. But the mental image we use to think of X need not be mental pictures of X. This is a point made explicitly in relation to spiritual, unpicturable, entities like God. But it is true of picturable things too. Very commonly, when we think of things in their absence, the mental images used are the *words*, the imagined sounds and shapes of words in our fragmentary inner monologues.

Shut your eyes and think to yourself 'water is H_2O'. The words which echo in the silence of your imagination are *phantasmata*, imagined sounds. Without some such mental event as the sub-vocal mouthing of those words, there would be no reason to say you were thinking that thought, *now*. But what makes it a *thought*, and *that particular thought*, is of course the meaning of the words and symbols. It is the understanding the words, the knowing the meaning, which makes what you do an act of *intellect*. The relation here between intellect and phantasm is necessary for any intellectual thought whatever, however universal. The 'reflection upon phantasms' which we mentioned above adds something extra, in the case of knowledge of individuals. Thus, if the thought you think in silence is 'Mrs Thatcher was a better administrator than President Reagan but not as good an actor' there is an extra role of sensory memory involved to attach the thoughts of Thatcher and Reagan to the individuals in question. We might put Aquinas's thought into Fregean mode by saying: Sense is a matter of intellect, reference is a matter of imagination.

For Aquinas the real object of all human knowledge is form. This is true both of sensory acquaintance and of intellectual understanding. The senses perceive the accidental forms of objects that are appropriate to each modality: with our eyes we see the colours and shapes of objects, with our noses we perceive their smells; colours, shapes and smells are accidental forms.

These are individual forms: the smell of *this rose*. Substantial form is not perceived by the senses, but grasped by the intellect. Material things are composed of matter and form: the individuality of a parcel of matter is not something that can be grasped by the intellect. The intellect can grasp what makes Socrates human, but not what makes him Socrates.

If Plato was wrong, as Aquinas thought he was, then there is not, outside the mind, any such thing as human nature as such: there is only the human nature of individual human beings such as Tom, Dick, and Harry. But because the humanity of individuals is form embedded in matter, it is not something which can, as such, be the object of pure intellectual thought. The agent intellect, on the basis of our experience of individual human beings, creates the intellectual object, humanity as such; but in order to conceive the humanity of Tom, Dick, or Harry we need to call in aid the imagination and the senses.

Aquinas's account of the agent intellect is complicated, and in some details obscure; but he is surely correct to attribute to human beings a special abstractive power unshared by other animals. In order to possess the type of concepts which we use to refer to and describe the objects of our experience it is not sufficient merely to have sensory experience. Children see, hear, and smell dogs before they acquire the concept *dog* and learn that the word 'dog' can be applied to labradors, poodles, and dachshunds but not to cats and sheep; they feel pricks and aches and cramps long before they acquire the concept *pain*. In mastering language the family baby acquires concepts which are beyond the reach of the family pets which are living in much the same sensory environment.

If the agent intellect is the capacity to acquire intellectual concepts and beliefs, the receptive intellect is the ability to retain and employ the concepts and beliefs thus acquired. It is the storehouse of ideas; the initially blank page on which the agent intellect writes. At any given moment in a human being's history there will be a repertoire of intellectual skills acquired and a stock of opinions and knowledge possessed. That repertoire and that stock make up the contents of the receptive intellect. Sometimes Aquinas's language makes us think of the receptive intellect as a kind of spiritual matter which takes on new forms as a thinker acquires new ideas. He warns us against taking this too seriously:

but it is because of the Aristotelian comparison that to this day we speak of being *informed* about a matter and call the gaining of knowledge the acquisition of *information*.

Sense-perception, according to Aquinas, was, like the acquisition of intellectual information, a matter of the reception of forms in an immaterial manner. The sense takes in the colour of gold, without the gold. Forms thus received by the sense were stored in the fancy, and can be reshuffled to produce images of whatever we care to think about.

Aquinas's account of the relation between sense and imagination is, in various ways, unsatisfactory; but he had a clear grasp of the relationship between the intellect and the imagination when thought takes place in mental images or in subvocal speech. In such cases it is not the imagery that gives content to the intellectual thought; it is the intellect that gives meaning to the imagery— whether imagined words or mental pictures—by using it in a certain way and in a certain context. In the book of our thoughts, it is the intellect that provides the text; the mental images are only illustrations.

Sense-perception and intellectual thought are, then, both cases of the reception of forms in a more or less immaterial manner in the mind. In both perception and thought a form exists, as Aquinas puts it, 'intentionally'. When I see the redness of the setting sun, redness exists intentionally in my vision; when I think of the roundness of the earth, roundness exists in my intellect. In each case the form exists without the matter to which it is joined in reality: the sun itself does not enter into my eye, nor does the earth, with all its mass, move into my intellect.

Suppose I think of a horse. There are two questions which a philosopher might ask about this thought. First: what makes it a thought *of a horse?* Second, what makes it *my* thought? Aquinas's answer to the first question is that it is the very same thing as makes a real horse a horse: namely, the form of horse. The form exists, individualized and materialized, in the real horse; it exists, universal and immaterial, in my mind. In the one case it has natural existence; in the other case it has intentional existence.

Aquinas's answer to the second question is less clear cut. There is nothing in the content of a thought that makes it one person's thought rather than another. Innumerable people besides myself believe that two and two make four: when I believe this, what makes the belief *my* belief? In response to the question, Aquinas points to the connection between the intellectual content of the thought (which is universal) and the mental images in which it is embodied (which are peculiar to me). The validity of the answer clearly depends upon the theory of the single human form: the intellectual and sensory activity must both be exercises of a single set of abilities if the thought is to be attached to a person.

If Aquinas's answer is to be fully convincing it needs to be spelt out more fully than he ever does. But what is notable is that unlike later philososphers he does not relate thought to a self or ego. This, in my view, is all to the good: the belief that each of us has a self is a piece of philosophers' nonsense. I and myself are one; myself is what I am, not a self which I have. If it were, then what in heaven's name is the I who has the self? My self is not a part of me, not even a most elusive, intimate, and precious part of me. The belief in a self which is different from the human being whose self it is is a grammatical illusion generated by the reflexive pronoun. It is as if a philosopher was puzzled what the property of 'own-ness' was which my own room possesses in addition to the property of being mine. When, outside philosophy, I talk about myself, I am simply talking about the human being, Anthony Kenny; and my self is nothing other than myself. It is a philo-sophical muddle to allow the space which differentiates 'my self' from 'myself' to generate the illusion of a mysterious meta-physical entity distinct from, but obscurely linked to, the human being whom you might meet and talk to.

The grammatical error which is the essence of the theory of the self is a deep error and one which is not generated by mistaken grammar alone. The illusion has a number of different roots, of which the most important are the epistemological root and the psychological root.

The epistemological root of the notion of the self is Cartesian scepticism. Descartes, in the *Meditations*, convinces himself that he can doubt whether the world exists and whether he has a body. He then goes on to argue, 'I can doubt whether I have a body; but I cannot doubt whether I exist; for what is this I which is doubting'. The 'I' must refer to something of which is body is no part, and hence to something which is no more than a part of the human being Descartes. The Cartesian ego is a substance whose essence is pure thought, the mind or *res cogitans*.

The psychological root of the notion of the self derives from the idea that imagination is an interior sense. The self, as conceived in the empiricist tradition of Locke, is the subject of inner sensation. The self is the eye of inner vision, the ear of inner hearing, or rather, it is the mythical possessor of both inner eye and inner ear and whatever other inner organs of sensation may be fantasized.

The self, to be sure, is a topic which has fascinated other people beside philosophers. Gerard Manley Hopkins, in an often quoted passage of his treatise on St Ignatius's spiritual exercises, wrote as follows:

We may learn that all things are created by consideration of the world without or of ourselves the world within. The former is the consideration commonly dwelt on, but the latter takes on the mind more hold. I find myself both as man and as myself something most determined and distinctive, at pitch, more distinctive and higher pitched than anything else I see; I find myself with my pleasures and pains, my powers and my experiences, my deserts and guilt, my shame and sense of beauty, my dangers, hopes, fears and all my fate, more important to myself than anything I see . . .

And this is much more true when we consider the mind; when I consider my selfbeing, my consciousness and feeling of myself, that taste of myself, of *I* and *me* above and in all things, which is more distinctive than the taste of ale or alum, more distinctive than the smell of walnutleaf or camphor, and is incommunicable by any means to another man (as when I was a child I used to ask myself: What must it be to be someone else?). Nothing else in nature comes near this unspeakable stress of pitch, distinctiveness, and selving, this selfbeing of my own. Nothing explains it or resembles it, except so far as this, that other men to themselves have the same feeling. But this only multiplies the phenomena to be explained so far as the cases are like and do resemble. But to me there is no resemblance: searching nature I taste *self* but at one tankard, that of my own being.

Like Hopkins, David Hume looked within to find his self; notoriously Hume's most diligent introspection failed to reveal any such thing.

When I enter most intimately into what I call *myself* I always stumble on some particular perception or other, of heat or cold, light or shade, love or hatred, pain or pleasure. I never catch *myself* at any time without a perception, and never can observe anything but the perception.

The self is everywhere—as for Hopkins—or it is nowhere—as for Hume. This is because the self is a mythical entity. A taste of which everything tasted would not be a taste, since taste is a faculty of discrimination; a self which is perceived no matter what is perceived is no better than a self which is not perceived at all.

There is, of course, such a thing as self-knowledge; but it is not knowledge of a self. When I know myself, what I know is myself, not my self. But even without the surd of the self, self-knowledge is a difficult philosophical topic: and it is instructive to see the difficulties which it presents for Aquinas even though he is blessedly free from belief in a mythical self.

Aquinas's general theory of knowledge, we have seen, makes intellectual knowledge of any individual problematic. The reason is that the principle of individuation for material objects is individual matter; and our intellect understands by abstracting ideas from such matter. But what is abstracted from individual matter is universal. So our intellect is not directly capable of knowing anything which is not universal. If this is so, how can I have intellectual knowledge of myself? According to Aquinas I am neither a disembodied spirit nor a universal, but a human being, an individual material object. As an individual material substance, it seems, I can be no fit object for intellectual cognition.

As we have seen, Aquinas solved the problem in relation to other individuals by appealing to the sensory context of thought. My relationship to other individuals is intellectual, because I can apply to them the universal ideas which are expressed in our common language; it is sensory because only the context of sense-experience enables us to attach the universal predicates to the individual subjects.

Aquinas's theory here seemed unnecessarily complicated to his successor Duns Scotus and to other philosophers, medieval and modern, who have believed in individuating essences, or, to use the Scotist term, haecceities. A haecceity is sufficiently like a form to be at home in the intellect: for Scotus the intellect can grasp the individuality of a thing by taking in its haecceity along with its universal form. But I believe that St Thomas was right to reject the notion of individuating essences: they are a misguided attempt to combine the logical features of form and matter, of predicate and subject. St Thomas did, of course, believe in individual essences—the essence of Peter is numerically distinct from the essence of Paul—but individual essences are not individuating essences. Peter's essence is a human nature individuated by being the essence *of Peter*; it is not Peter who is individuated by some Petreity which is his essence.

If there were forms such as Petreity it would be as true of them as it is of forms of other kinds that one cannot individuate by the accumulation of form: it must remain logically possible for more than one thing to possess identical Petreities. Once again, this thought received eloquent expression by Hopkins, that most engaging and intrepid Scotist.

In the world, besides natures, or essences, or inscapes, and the selves, supposits, or hypostases, or, in the case of rational natures, persons that wear and 'fetch' or instance them, there is still something else—fact or fate. For let natures be A,B,...Y,Z, and supposits or selves a,b,...y,z: then if a is capable of A,B,...Y,Z (singly or together) and receives, say A, if b capable of the same receives A and if c capable of the same receives M, so that we have aA, bA, cM, these combinations are three arbitrary or absolute facts, not depending on any essential relation between a & A, b & A or c & M but on the will of the Creator. Further, a & b are in the same nature A. But a uses it well and is saved, b ill and is damned; these are two facts, two fates, not depending on the relation between a and b on the one hand and A on the other. Now as the difference of the fact and fate does not depend on A, which is the same for both, it must depend on a and b. So that selves are from the first intrinsically different. (*Journals and Papers*, ed. House, OUP, 1959, p. 146)

In other words, Scotist selves have to be individuated in advance of possessing the haecceities which individuate them. But that takes away the point of introducing haecceities in the first place. The *reductio ad absurdum* is complete.

By contrast, Aquinas's theory of intellectual knowledge of the individual is basically sound, and much preferable to its Scotist alternatives, old and new. It is, however, bound up with a dubious theory of the imagination as an inner sense. Aquinas seems to have thought that an inner sense differed from an outer sense principally in having an organ and an object inside the body instead of outside the body; and he sometimes writes implicitly—as Descartes was later to write explicitly—as if mental images were images in the brain. This seems to me an error; but I believe that one can tacitly correct these errors and be left with a theory which is both philosophically defensible and recognizably Thomist.

The situation changes, however, if we turn from knowledge of other individuals to knowledge of oneself. Here, I shall claim, the weaknesses of St Thomas's account of the phantasm affect the substance of the theory; and once the account is adjusted to remove the weaknesses, the theory of self-knowledge reveals itself as inadequate.

A criticism can be levelled at Aquinas which he himself levelled at Averroes. Averroes, St Thomas says, regarded the receptive intellect as a separate substance, and 'said that the thoughts of that separate substance were my thoughts or your thoughts to the extent that that possible intellect was linked to me or to you by the phantasms which are in me or you'. The way in which this happened was thus explained by Averroes.

The intellectual idea which is united to the possible intellect as its form and act has two subjects—one the phantasm, the other the receptive intellect. Thus the receptive intellect is linked to us through its form by means of the phantasm; and that is how, when the possible intellect thinks, the human being thinks.

This account, St Thomas says, is empty. He gives three reasons against it, of which the third is the clinching one. Let us allow, he says, that one and the same idea is both a form of the possible intellect and is simultaneously in the phantasm; just as a wall's looking blue to me is the very same thing as my seeing the blue-ness of the wall.

But the coloured wall, whatever sense impression it makes on the sight, is seen, not seeing; it is the animal with the visual faculty on which the impression is made that is doing the seeing. But this is the alleged kind of link between the possible intellect and the human being in whom are the phantasms whose ideas are in the possible intellect—the same kind of link as that between the coloured wall and the sight on which the colour is impressed. But the wall doesn't see, but is seen; so it would follow not that the human being thought, but that his phantasms were thought of by the possible intellect.

St Thomas's criticism of Averroes seems to me inescapable; but does his own account of knowledge of self fare any better?

St Thomas in fact gives more than one account of self-knowledge. His fullest, and most considered answer to the question
how the intellect knows its own essence is summarized thus:

> It is not by its essence but by its acts that the intellect knows itself. And
> this in two ways. First, in particular, as when Socrates or Plato perceives
> himself to have an intellectual soul from the fact that he perceives himself
> thinking intellectual thoughts. Secondly, in general, as when we consider
> the nature of the human mind from the nature of the intellectual activity.

Here 'Socrates' intellect knows itself' is glossed, in conformity
with Aristotelian orthodoxy 'Socrates perceives himself to have
an intellectual soul'; and the theorem stated is an instance of the
axiom that faculties are known by their actions.

Thus, Aquinas says, everything is known so far as actual; and
the perfection of the intellect is its own immanent action. The
human intellect is not, like the divine intellect, identical with its
own act, nor does it have, like an angelic intellect, its own essence
as its primary object. Its primary object is the nature of material
things.

> Therefore, what is first known by the human intellect is this object; then,
> in the second place, the act by which the object is known is itself known;
> and finally, by way of the act, the intellect, of which the act of thinking is
> the perfection, is itself known.

So the intellect knows itself by knowing its own acts. But what
makes these acts—thoughts, exercises of concepts and beliefs—
the acts of an individual? We must put to St Thomas the question
he put to Averroes.

Aquinas was right to say, against Averroes, that my thoughts
are *my* thoughts because they are thoughts of the intellectual soul
which is individuated by my body. But when we ask for an
account of what makes the soul *that* soul, what is its relation to
my body which individuates it, we seem to be given no satisfact-
ory answer. For the mind (the possible intellect) is the locus of
universal ideas, concepts, and beliefs; there is nothing in their
content which relates them to this body. And the way in which
the body is related to the thoughts is not by being an instrument in
their acquisition or exercise. St Thomas is anxious to say that
thought is an activity of the soul alone, and that the soul, having
an independent activity, is capable also of independent existence,
as an incorruptible substance in its own right.

The way in which the body is involved in intellectual thought, for Aquinas, is simply that my beliefs are acquired and employed with the aid of phantasms generated by my brain. But if so, the body is necessary for intellectual activity not in order to provide the mind with an instrument, but only to provide the mind with an object—phantasms being, in one sense of the word 'object', the object of the intellect's activity.

But if this is correct, then my body is related to my thought only in a relation of efficient causality—as Leonardo is related to the Mona Lisa, or as the blue wall is related to my vision. And this, as Aquinas said against Averroes, is not enough. Leonardo does not see the painting he left behind, nor does the wall see its colour.

What is the correct account of the relation of the body to thought? Aquinas is right to say that my thoughts are *my* thoughts because they are thoughts of the mind which is the mind of my body. Where he goes wrong is in his account of what it is to be the mind of a particular body. The correct answer is that a mind is the mind of the body whose actions *express* that mind's thoughts. My thoughts are the thoughts which find expression in the words and actions of my body; your thoughts are the thoughts which find expression in what is done by your body. It is by looking to see whose hand wrote certain words, whose lips formed certain sounds, that we decide *whose* thoughts are expressed in writings on paper or sounds in the air. It is by observing the performance of Socrates' body that we discover what intellectual skills, or moral virtues, Socrates possesses. And this is not a contingent matter—it is not an inductive procedure we adopt to discover the contents of a mind by observing the behaviour of a body. The relevant bodily behaviour is, in Wittgenstein's words, a criterion for the possession of the mental skills and dispositions.

In our own case, of course, we do not have to use criteria to discover what our thoughts are. As St Thomas says, we perceive ourselves to think. I know *what* I am thinking, and I know that it is I who am thinking, without needing to base this judgement on criteria. But *what* I know when I know that I have a certain thought is the *same* as what others know when they know what I am thinking; and *what* they know and what I know is something intrinsically linked to bodily criteria.

But the link with bodily criteria is not the crude and simple one of behaviourist fantasy. Much of our thought takes place in private meditation and finds no bodily expression. (We may be grateful for this: a world in which everyone always expressed their thoughts would be noisy, boring, and cruel.) So the question remains: what is the relation to my body of the thoughts which I think silently in the privacy of my imagination—that is to say, the phantasms which St Thomas takes as the crucial link between body and mind in thought?

It is no doubt true, as St Thomas says, that the occurrence of phantasms is due, causally, to events in the brain. But that causal link is contingent and not necessary, and it is not enough to make the thoughts *thought by me*, as St Thomas himself said in his polemic against Averroes.

The truth seems to be that what makes my unexpressed thoughts my thoughts is that they are thoughts which, if they found expression, would be expressed by my body (this body). It is I who would have to answer the question 'a penny for thoughts' by someone who wished to know what I was thinking; it is to this body the request must be addressed.

What *sense* the thoughts in my mind have depends on mastery of the language in which they occur, in my decoding of the symbols and imagery in which they are embodied. What *reference* they have depends on the history of *this body*, making the links between the current image and the remembered events which provide the context for the reflection upon phantasms. The very fact that they are unexpressed is something which depends on my will. As we grow from babyhood, expressed thoughts come first; the repression of their public expression is a social skill learned later with difficulty as inculcated by parents. While unspoken thoughts are episodic in that they are datable events (like a pang of hunger), they are also dispositional in that (again like a pang of hunger) they are defined by the kind of expression to which they have an intrinsic relationship. So even in our most secret thoughts the relationship between mind and body is more than the mere causal interaction which St Thomas's theory suggests. The notion of expression, not that of causation, is the key to the mind—body relationship. We must add Wittgenstein to Aquinas if we are to save Aquinas from falling despite himself into the arms of Averroes.

Let us return, finally, to the Oxford condemnation of Aquinas. It might well seem, initially, that the question whether in human beings there were multiple forms or only a single intellectual soul was something only peripheral to St Thomas's psychology, and of little interest to twentieth-century philosophy. But we have now seen how the question of the relationship between the intellectual and the sensory powers permeates every aspect of St Thomas's philosophy of the mind and its relation to the body. Moreover, the condemned propositions link up with present-day concerns about the nature of personal identity and with currently debated issues in medical ethics.

At the present time some philosophers regard memory as the key to personal identity; others see bodily continuity as its essence, while others again present theories which use both memory and bodily continuity as criteria. Those who separate personal identity from bodily identity take the side of those medievals who argued for the plurality of forms; those who identify the two in effect subscribe to the thesis for which St Thomas was condemned.

The questions debated in Oxford in 1277 are not mere abstract issues of no practical relevance. They connect with fundamental problems about the beginning and end of individual human life. What is the right way to conceptualize the continuity between a foetus and a baby? Should the continuance of vegetative function in an unconscious human body be taken as an indication of the permanence of a rational soul bearing the rights of persons? Taking sides in the medieval debate goes hand in hand with the approach to be adopted in answering these difficult questions.

In 1325 the Bishop of Paris proclaimed that the censure his university had passed in 1277 had no canonical value so far as it concerned St Thomas. In 1914 Pope Pius X listed as a thesis which was safe and sound to be taught in Catholic schools, 'The same rational soul is united to the body in such a way that it is its one and only substantial form, and through it a human being is animal, living, bodily, and substantial.'

Rome and Paris have withdrawn their initial condemnation of Aquinas. Only Oxford, so far as I know, has not yet done so. In presenting his views in this chapter, therefore, I may perhaps have rendered myself liable to lose my MA.

Duns Scotus on Freewill

It is now generally agreed that Scotus made important innovations in the theory of modality. I wish in this essay to examine in detail the passages which contain these innovations; they come from his discussion of the relation between divine foreknowledge and contingency in human actions, and in particular, from his treatment, in that context, of certain theorems about the relation between time and necessity contained in the ninth chapter of Aristotle's *De Interpretatione*.

Scotus's fullest treatment of the issues is found in distinction 39 of the *Opus Oxoniense*, his commentary, delivered as Oxford lectures, on the Sentences of Peter Lombard. The text is found in volume vi of the Vatican edition, the volume which contains the *Ordinatio*, or authorial revision, of these lectures. However, as these particular distinctions were not redacted by Scotus himself, they appear in an appendix to the volume, reconstructed from the *Reportatio* or student's notes of the course. It is from this which most of my texts for discussion will be drawn. There is a parallel discussion in the *Lectura*, volume xvi of the Vatican edition.[1]

Scotus's treatment of the question whether God has knowledge of the future begins with a pair of difficulties drawn from the *De Interpretatione*. Chapter 9 of that book has been the object of extensive scholarly discussion, both in the Middle Ages and in the last few decades, and it cannot be said that there is any consensus on its interpretation. It is clear, however, that while Aristotle accepts that it is necessary that there will either be a sea battle tomorrow or not be a sea battle tomorrow, he denies that it is in the same way necessary that there will be a sea battle tomorrow, or that it is in the same way necessary that there will not be a sea battle tomorrow. Some commentators believe he

---

[1] Page references are given to these volumes of the Vatican edn.

is saying that a proposition such as 'there will be a sea battle tomorrow' lacks a truth-value altogether; others think that he is prepared to allow that such a proposition is—as the case may be—true, and is merely denying that it is a necessary truth.

In the Middle Ages some authors, following Boethius, took up a third position, which is not altogether clear, but which appears to be somewhere between the two positions just stated. These authors said that future-tensed propositions about contingent matters did indeed possess a truth-value, but lacked a determinate truth-value. Such seems to have been the position of Aquinas, though I am not aware that he ever made sufficiently clear the difference between determinate truth and necessary truth. The terminology is taken over by Scotus. He puts the question whether God has determinate knowledge of futures, and gives as his *videtur quod non*: according to Aristotle in the *De Interpretatione* there is no determinate truth in future contingents; therefore they cannot be known, for knowledge requires determinate truth (xvi. 481).

It is common ground among commentators that Aristotle's thesis about future contingents, whatever its precise form, is intended to enable us to reject arguments for fatalism. Fatalism is the doctrine that whatever comes to pass comes to pass of necessity; and it is obviously false because if it were true deliberation and effort would be pointless. Scotus invokes this argument as an objection, not just to fatalism, but to the thesis that God knows the future: according to Aristotle, he says, deliberation and effort would be rendered pointless if there were determinate truth about future contingent matters.

A third thesis of Aristotle's which Scotus discusses in this context is the thesis that what is, necessarily is, when it is. This is taken, by Aquinas among others, to mean that the present has a necessity which the future has not. It is this which enables Aquinas to reconcile divine foreknowledge with sublunary contingency: in eternity God sees as present what is future to us, and because it is present as he sees it, it has the necessity which is required for knowability. Scotus, as we shall see, takes Aristotle's dictum in quite a different way.

Scotus places in the centre of the problem of foreknowledge and freedom not necessity, but possibility. In addition to the familiar Aristotelian texts he presents another, less familiar, difficulty against the thesis of divine foreknowledge of human free actions.

The following argument, he says, is valid: God believes I will sit tomorrow; but I will not sit tomorrow; therefore God is mistaken. Therefore the following argument also is valid: God believes I will sit tomorrow; but I can not sit tomorrow; therefore God can be mistaken. This assumes the validity of the schema: If p and q entail r, then p and possibly q entail possibly r.[2]

It is in solving this difficulty that Scotus introduces his most interesting modal innovations. Before setting out his own position, he rejects other attempts to reconcile foreknowledge with contingency, including that of Aquinas. Essentially, his argument goes that whatever is present to God cannot be genuinely future: the way things appear to God is the way they really are.[3] The way to approach the problem is not by an analysis of divine vision, but through the notion of freedom, human and divine.

Like Aristotle, Scotus believes that the existence of contingency is so obvious as neither to need nor permit of any genuine proof. Those who deny contingency, he says, should be put to torture until they admit that it is possible for them not to be tortured. What we need is an analysis of how contingency is caused by the will.

Scotus attributes to the human will a threefold freedom. 'I say that the will, insofar as it is first act, is free for opposite acts. It is also free, by means of those opposite acts, for the opposite objects

---

[2]   Ad secundam quaestionem arguo quod non:

Quia sequitur 'Deus novit me sessurum cras, et non sedebo cras, ergo Deus decipitur', igitur, a simili, sequitur 'Deus novit me sessurum cras, et possum non sedere cras, ergo Deus potest decipi'. Prima est manifesta, quia credens illud quod non est in re, decipitur; probo—ex hoc—quod consequentia teneat, quia sicut ad duas de inesse sequitur conclusio de inesse, ita ex una de inesse et altera de possibili sequitur conclusio de possibili. (vi. 402)

[3]   Item, si effectus habet esse in se ipso respectu causae primae, simpliciter est in se, quia respectu nullius habet verius esse: unde illud quod dicitur tale respectu causae primae, simpliciter potest dici tale. Si ergo aliquid futurum sit in actu respectu Dei, ergo simpliciter est in actu; ergo impossibile est ipsum posterius poni in actu.

Praeterea, si sessio mea futura (non tantum quantum ad entitatem quam habet in esse cognoscibili, sed quam habet in esse existentiae) est nunc praesens aeternitati, ergo nunc est producta in illo esse a Deo, nam nihil a Deo habet esse in fluxu temporis nisi sit productum a Deo secundum illud esse; sed istam sessionem Deus producet (vel animam Antichristi, quod idem est); ergo illud quod iam ab ipso productum est, iterum producetur in esse, et ita bis producetur in esse. (vi. 410)

to which it tends, and, further, for the opposite effects it produces.' This suggests the following instances: a free man can
either love Caesar or hate Caesar; he can love Caesar or love
Brutus; and he can kill Caesar or save Caesar. But Scotus does
not give instances (except for love and hatred, in *Lectura*), and it is
not altogether easy to grasp the distinctions he is making. He goes
on to say that the first freedom involves imperfection, since it
involves change, such as the change from loving to hating; and
the third freedom is inessential, since the will could remain free
even if impotent to bring about effects in the world. The essence of
freedom is the second one: the relationship to opposite objects: to
will X or not X.

When we have a case of free action, this freedom is accompanied by an obvious power to opposites, *una potentia ad opposita
manifesta*. True, the will can have no power to will X and not-
will X at the same time—that would be nonsense—but there is in
the will a power to will after not willing, or to a succession of
opposite acts. That is to say that while A is willing X at time t, A
can not-will X at time t + 1. This, he says, is the *manifesta potentia*,
the obvious power to do a different kind of act at a later time.

But, Scotus says, there is another, not obvious power, which is
without any temporal succession: *tamen est alia, non ita manifesta,
absque omni successione*. Scotus illustrates this kind of power by
imagining a case in which a created will existed only for a single
instant. In that instant it could only have a single volition, but
even that volition would not be necessary, but be free. The lack of
succession involved in this kind of freedom is most obvious in the
case of the imagined momentary will, but it is in fact there all the
time. That is, that while A is willing X at t, not only does A have
the power to not-will X at t + 1, but also the power to not-will X at
t, at that very moment. This is a very explicit innovation, the
discovery of this non-manifest, or we might say occult, power.[4]

---

[4] De secundo: eo quod istam libertatem concomitatur una potentia ad opposita
manifesta, licet enim non sit in ea potentia ad simul velle et non velle (quia hoc
nihil est), tamen est in ea potentia ad velle post non velle sive ad successionem
actuum oppositorum; et ista potentia est manifesta in omnibus mutabilibus, ad
successionem oppositorum in eis.

Tamen est et alia (non ita manifesta), absque omni successione. Ponendo enim
voluntatem creatam tantum habere esse in uno instanti, et quod ipsa in illo instanti
habeat hanc volitionem, non necessario tunc habet eam. Probatio: si enim in illo
instanti haberet eam necessario, cum non sit causa nisi in illo instanti quando

Scotus carefully distinguishes this power from logical possibility; it is something which accompanies logical possibility but is not identical with it. It is not simply the fact that there would be no contradiction in A's not willing X at this very moment, it is something over and above—a real active power—and it is the heart of human freedom.[5]

The sentence 'This will, which is willing X, can not-will X' can be taken in two ways. Taken *in sensu compositionis* it means that 'This will, which is willing X, is not-willing X' is possibly true; and that is false. Taken *in sensu divisionis*, as meaning that this will which is now willing X at t has the power of not-willing X at $t + 1$, it is obviously true.

But what of 'This will, which is willing X at t, can not-will X at t'? Here too, in accordance with Scotus's innovation, we can distinguish between the composite sense and the divided sense. It is not the case that it is possible that this will is simultaneously willing X at t and not-willing X at t. But it is true that it is possible that not-willing X at time t might inhere in this will which is actually willing X at time t (though of course, if it did, willing X would not be doing so).[6]

causaret eam, ergo simpliciter voluntas—quando causaret—necessario causaret; non enim modo est contingens causa quia praeexistebat ante istud instans in quo causat (et tunc 'ut praeexistens' potuit causare vel non causare), quia sicut hoc ens quando est, est necessarium vel contingens, ita causa quando causat, tunc causat necessario vel contingenter. Ex quo ergo in isto instanti causat hoc velle: et non necessario, ideo contingenter. Est ergo haec potentia causae 'ad oppositum eius quod causat' sine successione. (vi. 417–18)

[5] Hanc etiam potentiam realem activam (priorem naturaliter ipso quod producit) concomitatur potentia logica, quae est non-repugnantia terminorum. Voluntati enim ut actus primus, etiam quando producit hoc velle, non repugnat oppositum velle: tum quia causa contingens est, respectu effectus, et ideo non repugnat sibi oppositum in ratione effectus; tum quia ut subiectum est, contingenter se habet ad istum actum ut informat, quia subiecto non repugnat oppositum sui 'accidentis per accidens'. (vi. 418)

[6] Ex isto secundo patet tertium, scilicet distinctio huius propositionis 'voluntas volens *a*, potest non velle *a*'. Haec enim in sensu compositionis falsa est, ut significetur possibilitas huius compositionis 'voluntas volens *a*, non vult *a*'; vera est in sensu divisionis, ut significetur possibilitas ad opposita successive, quia voluntas volens pro *a* potest non velle pro *b*.

Sed si etiam accipiamus propositionem de possibili unientem extrema pro eodem instanti, puta istam 'voluntas non volens aliquid pro *a*, potest velle illud pro *a*' adhuc ista est distinguenda secundum compositionem et divisionem: et in sensu compositionis falsa, scilicet quod sit possibilitas quod ipsa sit simul volens pro *a* et non volens pro *a*; sensus divisionis verus, scilicet ut significetur quod illi voluntati cui inest 'velle pro *a*', possit inesse 'non velle pro *a*'. (vi. 419)

If the possibility of not-willing X remains in the will at the very moment at which it is willing X, then it seems that Scotus cannot accept Aquinas's view that the present is always necessary in a way that the future is not. Accordingly, he has to give a different interpretation of the dictum of the *De Interpretatione* that what is, when it is, is necessary.

There are three ways of interpreting this dictum. (1) Necessarily, while S is P, S is P. (2) S is necessarily P-while-P. (3) While S is P, S is necessarily P. Taken in the first two ways the dictum is undoubtedly true; and there is no need to interpret 'necessarily' in any terms other than those of logical necessity.

What of the dictum on the third interpretation? In the Aristotelian tradition, this is on the face of it not always true. I am alive, but I am not necessarily alive; I might drop dead at any moment. Only of beings like the sun and stars can it be said that while they exist, they exist necessarily.

However, Aristotle was interpreted by Aquinas and others as being committed to the view that, if it is now time *t*, if S is P at *t*, then S is necessarily P at *t*. It is at this point that Scotus innovates. If I am freely sitting now, there is no sense in which it is necessary that I am sitting now. For I have, at the very same moment, the power not to sit.

But if I am sitting now, and at this very same moment I have the power not to sit, does that not mean that I have the power to sit and not sit at the same time? Scotus puts this objection, and gives an answer to it. Scotus is right to say that the exercise, at *t*, of the power to do X does not take away the power not to do X. But he is wrong to say that it is compatible with the power not to do X at *t*, for there is no such power.[7]

---

[7] Tunc dico quod non sequitur 'potest velle hoc in *a*, et potest nolle hoc in *a*, ergo potest velle et nolle in *a*'. quia potest esse potentia ad utrumlibet oppositorum disiunctim pro aliquo instanti, etsi non ad ambo illa simul; quia sicut est possibilitas ad unum illorum, ita est ad non esse alterius,—et e converso sicut ad reliquum ita ad non esse istius. Non ergo simul ad esse huius et illius opposita, quia possibilitas ad simultatem non esset nisi esset ad ambo concurrentia in eodem instanti, quod non habetur per hoc quod ad utrumque divisim est potentia pro illo instanti.

Exemplum huius apparet in permanentibus: 'Hoc corpus potest esse in hoc loco in *a* instanti, et illud corpus potest esse in eodem loco in *a* instanti igitur ista duo corpora possunt esse simul in *a* instanti' non sequitur; ita enim potest hoc corpus esse ibi, quod potest illud corpus non ese ibi (et e converso), et ideo non sequitur 'si potentia est ad utrumque pro eodem—sive instanti sive loco—ergo ad ambo', sed

His solution involves a denial that 'I can do X at t and I can do Y at t' entails 'I can do X and Y at t'. This denial would be widely accepted, on the basis of the kinds of example suggested by Scotus (I can carry my suitcase and I can carry your suitcase; but I can't carry both together, they are too heavy). But other authors commonly would say that if I actually exercise the power to do X at t, then I cease to be able to do Y at t, if X and Y cannot be done simultaneously. If he is to avoid this, Scotus needs something more, which he provides only later.

Scotus applies this theory of the will to the divine will. His answer to the question how God knows future contingents is that he does so by his knowledge of his own will. Take a proposition such as 'there will be a sea battle on such and such a date'. When the divine mind considers this proposition in eternity, prior to any divine decision, it apprehends it, Scotus says, as neuter, just as I apprehend the proposition 'The total number of stars is an even number'. But after the decree of God's will the proposition begins to be determinately true, as it was not before. Once it thus becomes determinately true, it can be known by God. However, it remains a contingent truth, since the decrees of God's will are not necessary but contingent.

A number of questions arise about this. When Scotus says that, prior to the divine decree, the sea-battle proposition is neuter, does he mean that it is neither true nor false? That seems the most natural interpretation; on the other hand, it is not clear to me that 'the number of stars is even' was believed by Scotus to lack a truth-value, rather than to be merely undecidable. At all events, the distinction between neutrality and determinate truth seems to be one which holds only in the divine decision-procedure in eternity. On the basis of this passage, one could conclude that by the time any of the likes of us are around, the sea-battle propositions all have determinate truth, even though they lack necessity.

Surprisingly, however, Scotus goes on to maintain an asymmetry between future and past, and to defend a special determinacy of the present.

---

fallit quandocumque utrumlibet illlorum duorum excludit alterum. Ita etiam non sequitur 'possum tota die portare istum lapidem (sit portabile aliquid, adaequatum virtuti meae), et possum tota die portare illum lapidem, ergo possum simul portare ambos'; non sequitur, quia hic utrumque ad quod est potentia divisim, excludit reliquum. (vi. 424)

In present and past cases there is determinate truth, because one of the contradictories has been brought about; and if considered as brought about it is not in the power of its cause that it should be brought about or not brought about. It is true that it is in the power of the cause, considered as being prior by nature to its effect, to bring about or not bring about its effect; the same is not the case if the effect is considered as already brought into existence. But there is no such determination in the case of the future, because even if there is an intellect to which one side of the antiphasis is determinately true (or even if one side is determinately true in itself, even if there were no intellect grasping it), it is not beyond the power of the cause to bring about the opposite at that instant. And this degree of indeterminacy is enough for deliberation and effort; but if neither side were true, there would be no need for effort or deliberation. So one side's being future, while the other still has the power of coming about, presents no problem for deliberation and effort.[8]

This is clear enough, and would have been accepted by many pre-Scotist scholastics. But how is it to be reconciled with the innovation we have seen in Scotus? Surely Scotus has been claiming that not only in the case of the future eventuation of an effect, but even in the case of the actual exercise of a power, there remains the power for the opposite. Whereas others have said that the exercise of the power not to do X at t is extinguished by the performance of X at t, for Scotus the power is not extinguished, but only becomes latent or occult.

I am not sure how to solve this puzzle: no doubt the solution lies in working out a systematic distinction between determinacy and necessity. But for the clearest statement of Scotus's position we have to turn to the response which he gave to the objection stated earlier. He rejects the schema: If p and q entail r, then p and possibly q entail possibly r. In the case in point, he says, 'I can not sit tomorrow' affirms a power of the opposite

---

[8] In praesentibus quidem et praeteritis est veritas determinata, ita quod alterum extremum est positum,—et ut intelligitur positum, non est in potestate causae ut ponatur vel non ponatur, quia licet in potestate causae 'ut prior naturaliter est effectu' sit ponere effectum vel non ponere, non tamen ut effectus intelligitur iam positus in esse. Talis autem non est determinatio ex parte futuri, quia licet alicui intellectui sit una pars vera determinate (et etiam una pars sit vera in se, determinate, licet eam nullus intellectus apprehenderet), non tamen ita quin in potestate causae est pro illo instanti ponere oppositum. Et ista indeterminatio sufficit ad consiliandum et negotiandum; si neutra pars esset futura, non oporteret negotiari nec consiliari,—ergo quod altera pars sit futura, dum tamen reliqua possit evenire, non prohibet consiliationem et negotiationem. (vi. 432)

(of my eventual sitting): *non pro eodem instanti conjunctim, sed disjunctim.*[9]

What does this mean? The time indication—*cras*—is the same both in *Deus novit me sessurum cras* and in *possum non sedere cras*. I agree with Simo Knuuttila that what we have here is not an instant of time but an instant of nature, and an instant of nature is best understood as something like a possible world. At the same instant of time there can be more than one instant of nature, there may be several synchronic possibilities. These synchronic possibilities need not be compossible, as in the case in point: they are possible *disjunctim* (in different possible worlds) not *conjunctim* (in the same possible world).

While agreeing with Knuuttila that Scotus can be said, in a manner, to have invented possible worlds, I do not agree that this was a beneficent innovation. Like Ockham, I find Scotus's occult powers incomprehensible. But I do not think that the way to correct Scotus's mistake is to say that the power not to sit at *t* should be regarded as a power existing not at *t* (when I am sitting) but at *t* − 1, the last moment at which it was still open to me to be standing up at *t*. The right line to take is to say that powers, unlike their exercises, are not datable events.

For it to be true that I can swim now, it is necessary not only that I should know how to swim—now have the power to swim—there must also be some water about. I need the opportunity, as well as the power, to swim.

Scotus was right that an analysis of freedom involves an analysis of being able to do something at a specified time. But his analysis of this ability was hampered by his failure to distinguish between power and opportunity, and this led him into the unnecessary mystification of occult powers and instants of nature.

---

[9] Ad primum argumentum secundae quaestionis dico quod licet ad duas de inesse sequatur conclusio de inesse (non quidem syllogistice, quia est oratio non syllogistica, reducibilis in syllogismos multos), tamen ex una de inesse et altera de possibili nec syllogistice nec necessario sequitur conclusio de possibili; ratio est, quia 'falli' est rem opinari aliter esse quam sit, pro tunc pro quando creditur esse. Istud autem includitur in illis duabus praemissis de inesse, quarum altera significat istum credere hoc et reliqua negat hoc esse, et hoc pro eodem instanti,—et ideo sequitur conclusio de falli. Non sic autem ex alia parte, quia illa de inesse affirmat unum oppositum pro illo instanti, illa de possibili affirmat potentiam ad alterum oppositum, non pro eodem instanti conjunctim, sed disjunctim. (vi. 433–4)

It may be true, at *t* that I have the power to do *X*, without this meaning that I have the power to do-*X*-at-*t*. There may indeed be possibilities for things to happen at a certain time, and only at a certain time; but when that is so that is not due to the nature of the powers involved.

Scotus failed to distinguish between

At *t*, I can do *X*

a temporarily qualified statement which may be true of a power, and

I can do *X* at *t*,

which, unless the 'at *t*' is vacuous, must involve the notion of an opportunity. The occult power to do *X* at *t* is an amalgam of the two notions.

Scotus is right that

I can not-do-*X* at *t*

must be true if I am doing *X* at *t* freely. It is also true that if

I can do *X* at *t*

is true, then at *t* I must have the power to do *X*, and the opportunity to do *X* at *t*. But an opportunity is not an occult power of mine; it is more a matter of the states and powers of other things, and the compossibility of those states and powers with the exercise of my power.

Scotus is right to say that the exercise, at *t*, of the power to do *X* does not take away the power not to do *X*. But he is wrong to say that it is compatible with the power not to do *X* at *t*, for there is no such power.

It is also true that my *willing* to do *X* does not take away my opportunity not to do *X*. Equally, it is true that God's knowing that I will do *X* does not take away my opportunity not to do *X*. But in order to establish this there is no need for Scotus to bring in occult powers and instants of nature. The distinction between power and opportunity will achieve the task with a much slighter investment in controversial metaphysics.[10]

[10] See my *Will, freedom and Power* (Blackwell, 1975), 122–61.

8

Aristotle versus Descartes on Sensation

The dualism of Descartes continues to fascinate scholars. In 1996 and 1998 books appeared each bearing the title *Descartes's Dualism*, one by Gordon Baker and Katherine Morris (henceforth DDBM),[1] and the other by Marleen Rozemond (henceforth DDR).[2] The former tries to overturn the received interpretation of Descartes as a dualist; the latter is much more respectful of tradition, but seeks to adjust the standard perception of Descartes's system by relating it to the scholastic background of his age. Stimulated by these two books, I wish to examine one particular issue which is crucial to Cartesian dualism: Descartes's understanding of the nature of sensation.[3]

In giving his account of sensation and sense-perception a large part of the task which Descartes sets himself is to disambiguate the terms *sentir* (French) and *sentire* (Latin). He separates out a number of different senses in which these words can be used. But in making his distinctions Descartes does not see himself as simply drawing attention to an ambiguity in ordinary language. Ordinary language is the language of those who are thinking confused thoughts. What Descartes is doing is to bring out of obscurity into clarity different layers of content in sentences which contain *sentire* or *sentir* or verbs, such as *video* and *doleo*, for particular forms of sensation such as vision and pain.

The starting point, prior to Cartesian reflection, is the Aristotelian notion of sensation in which it is the activity of an ensouled

---

[1] London: Routledge, 1996.

[2] Cambridge, Mass.: Harvard University Press, 1998.

[3] In what follows references to Descartes are made by volume and page number to standard edns.: AT refers to *Œuvres de Descartes*, ed. Charles Adam and Paul Tannery (Paris: Vrin/CNRS, revised edn., 1964–76); CSM refers to *The Philosophical Writings of Descartes* trans. John Cottingham, Robert Stoothoff, and Dugald Murdoch, vols. i and ii (Cambridge: Cambridge University Press 1991), and CSMK to vol. iii, *The Correspondence*, by the same translators plus Anthony Kenny (1995).

organic body. In the sixth paragraph of the Second Meditation Descartes asks which of the activities of the soul (*quae animae tribuebam*) belong to him: 'Sense-perception (*sentire*)? This surely does not occur without a body, and besides, when asleep I have appeared to perceive through the senses many things which I afterwards realised I did not perceive through the senses at all' (AT vii. 27: CSM ii. 18). *Sentire*, in this passage, includes bodily function and is contrasted with *cogitatio* or thought. But this is a passage in the dialectical argument between the unreformed Descartes and the sceptical Descartes; it is the unreformed Descartes who is speaking, still thinking in Aristotelian terms ('anima' etc.), and with his ideas still confused, not yet fully purified by the discipline of the doubt and the Cogito.

Once Descartes has realized that he is a *res cogitans*, things become clearer. *Cogitatio* is no longer contrasted with *sensus*, but if we get a precise notion of what *sensus* is we realize that it is a kind of *cogitatio*.

It is the same I who has sensory perceptions, or is aware of bodily things as it were through the senses. For example, I am now seeing light, hearing a noise, feeling heat. But I am asleep, so all this is false. Yet I certainly seem to see, to hear, and to be warmed. This cannot be false; what is called 'sensing' is strictly just this (*hoc est proprie quod in me sentire appellatur*) and in this restricted sense of the term it is simply thinking. (AT vii. 29; CSM ii. 19).

Descartes here isolates the indubitable immediate experience, the seeming-to-see-a-light which cannot be mistaken. This datum of sensory consciousness is nothing other than a *cogitatio*, and it is this item that is common to both veridical and hallucinatory experience which is, for Descartes, 'sensation strictly so called'.

There are many passages in which Descartes lists sensation and sense-perception ('internal' and 'external' sensation, in his vocabulary) as species of thought. For instance, in the Second Replies he says 'all the operations of the will, the intellect, the imagination and the senses are thoughts' (AT vii. 160: CSM ii. 113). And in the *Principles*, 'thinking is to be identified here not merely with understanding, willing and imagining, but also with sensory awareness'. If I take 'I see' to refer to the actual sense or awareness of seeing, it relates to the mind 'which alone has the sensation or thought that it is seeing' (AT viii. 7: CSM i. 195). Later in the same work he says that if we are to perceive pain and colour clearly and distinctly we must regard them 'merely as sensations or thoughts'. A similar account of sensation and sense-perception is given in articles 17–25 of the first book of the Passions of the Soul (AT xi. 342–8: CSM i. 335–8). So here, from different periods of Descartes's life, we have, to contrast with the Aristotelian sense from which we started, a specific Cartesian sense of 'sensation': a *cogitatio* or immediate datum of consciousness.

But this is not the only thing which Descartes is prepared to call 'sensation'. This comes out most clearly in the passage of the Sixth Replies in which he spells out a three-stage account of the operation of sense-perception.

The first is limited to the immediate stimulation of the bodily organs by external objects; this can consist in nothing but the motion of the particles of the organs, and any change of shape and position resulting from this motion. The second grade comprises all the immediate effects produced in the mind as a result of its being united with a bodily organ which is affected in this way. Such effects include the perceptions of pain, pleasure, thirst, hunger, colours, sound, taste, smell, heat, cold and the like, which arise from the union and as it were the intermingling of mind and body, as explained in the Sixth Meditation. This third grade includes all the judgements about things outside us which we have been accustomed to make from our earliest years—judgements which are occasioned by the movements of these bodily organs. (AT vii. 436–7: CSM ii. 294–5)

He goes on to illustrate these three stages in the case of seeing a stick. (1) Rays of light reflected off the stick excite motions in my brain via the optic nerve. (2) In my mind there is the perception of light and colour. (3) I make judgements about the colour of the stick, and calculations about its size and distance. Now while Descartes thinks it is of prime importance to distinguish the intellectual judgement from the pure sensory perception, he is willing to call these third-stage judgements 'sensations'. It is thus that he glosses his own dictum that 'the certainty of the intellect is much greater than that of the senses': 'This means merely that when we are grown up the judgements which we make as a result of various new observations are more reliable than those which we formed without any reflection in our early childhood' (AT vii. 438: CSM i. 295).

In this passage, then, we meet a third sense of *sentire* in Descartes: the making of a judgement on the basis of a perception. It is important to distinguish this from the perception itself: both perceptions and judgements are thoughts (*cogitationes*), but the latter, unlike the former, are acts of the will, as Descartes explained in the Fourth Meditation (AT vii. 56 and 60: CSM ii. 39 and 41). It is by the exercise of the will—by refraining from precipitancy in judgement—that we proceed from the confusion of childhood to the clarity and distinctness which Cartesian discipline brings to our sense-perception.

These three senses do not exhaust the meaning of 'sensation' in Descartes. In the three-stage schema of the Sixth Replies the first stage consists of the mechanical disturbance caused in the body by the external stimulus. In at least one passage Descartes is prepared to call this purely physical event 'sensation'. Thus, in a letter to the Marquess of Newcastle, having explained how in animals the bones, nerves, muscles, and other bodily elements are sufficient, without thought, to give rise to all the movements we observe, so that there is no reason to attribute thought to them, he continues: 'Please note that I am speaking of thought, and not of life or sensation. I do not deny life to animals, since I regard it as consisting simply in the heat of the heart; and I do not even deny sensation, in so far as it depends on a bodily organ' (AT v. 277: CSMK 365). From the context it is clear that what is meant by sensation here are the bodily functions which, if they occurred in a human being, would be linked with sensation in the strict sense, that is to say, with the mental perception identified in the Second Meditation. Since he denies that animals have thoughts, Descartes is committed to denying that they have sensation in the strict sense; but in this passage he agrees that the equivalent bodily functions, occurring in a non-thinking animal, can be called 'sensation'—in an extended sense.

We can sum up as follows. In order to do justice to the texts we have considered, we need to recognize four senses of 'sensation' (*sentire*) in Descartes:

(A) Confused Aristotelian sense in which it is the act of an ensouled organic body.
(B) Primary Cartesian sense in which it means a pure mentalistic *cogitatio*.
(C) Secondary Cartesian sense in which it includes a judgement of the will (a different form of *cogitatio*).

(D) Secondary Cartesian sense in which it means a mechanistic *motio*, common to humans and animals.

In their book Baker and Morris attempt to reduce the Cartesian senses of 'sensation' to two. An expression such as 'seeing light' in one sense refers to something purely bodily, which animals too could exhibit; in another, rational, sense it means making the mental judgement that one sees light in the bodily sense. 'It seems to me that I see light' is understood to be equivalent to 'I judge that I see light', and it reports the fact that I am making (or have just made) that judgement. The judgement that I judge (have just judged) that I see light, etc. is an exercise of *conscientia* (the power to reflect on the operations of one's mind) which, in this particular case, 'cannot be false'. The criteria for seeing light in the bodily sense relate to the situation of the seer's body and its reactions to that situation; the criteria for rational seeing include such things as making the statement 'I see light' (see DDBM 72–4).

In terms of the schema above, the account of Baker and Morris conflates senses (B) and (C). It is incorrect to contend that the mental element, sensation in the primary Cartesian sense of the word, involves judgement. These authors misunderstand the way in which Descartes isolates the indubitable kernel of 'I see'. They think that in this sense to talk about seeing is to talk about the purely mental activity of making a judgement (e.g. 'It seems to me that I see light'). The reason that only human beings can be proved to see in this sense is, they believe, that only human beings can be proved to make judgements. But they are wrong to think that Descartes regards 'It seems to me that I see light' as a judgement.

It may seem natural to a twentieth-century philosopher to think that a sentence such as 'I seem to see a light' expresses a judgement. But for Descartes it is a thought which it is possible to have without making a judgement at all. This is precisely the position in which Descartes finds himself at the beginning of the Second Meditation. Purified by the discipline of the doubt, he refrains from making any judgements: but none the less he has all kinds of thoughts, including such thoughts as 'I seem to see a light'. The mere registering of a protocol of perception is not, for Descartes, a judgement. The first judgement to be made, in the Cartesian system, is *sum*; and this is the recognition not of a particular mode of the mind, but of the mental substance in which those modes inhere. When Descartes speaks of sensory judgements (as in the passages making use of sense (C)) he is talking not about the internal content of the sensations but of their relation to extra-mental reality. Thoughts such as 'I seem to see a light' come unbidden and are not under voluntary control; but judgement is something which is, in such cases, within our power to make or withhold. The whole strategy of the Fourth Meditation depends on a distinction between the thoughts of the intellect (which are in my mind whether I want them to be or not) and the judgement of the will—itself another kind of thought—from which I am free to abstain. A particularly full—but by no means exceptional—account of his position is given in the *Comments on a Broadsheet*:

I have stated that [the properties of the soul] reduce to two principal ones, of which one is the perception of the intellect and the other the deter-mination of the will. I saw that over and above perception, which is a prerequisite of judgement, we need affirmation and negation to deter-mine the form of the judgement, and also that we are often free to with-hold our assent, even if we perceive the matter in question. Hence I assigned the act of judging itself, which consists simply in assenting (i.e. in affirmation or denial) to the determination of the will rather than to the perception of the intellect. (AT viiiB. 363; CSM ii. 307)

Baker and Morris not only elide the distinction between percep-tion and judgement, they also assign a quite implausible content to the judgement. They are, of course, correct in saying that for Descartes, there is a purely mechanical element in seeing, which can occur in animals no less than in humans: for instance, the extremities of the optic nerves being moved by globules of the second element. But it is very strange to say, as they do, that 'I seem to see a light' expresses the judgement that this mechanical operation is taking place. The sense-experiences described in the Second Meditation occur in multitudes of people who have not the faintest idea of the physical mechanics of vision. Moreover, in saying that the content of 'I seem to see a light' may be that I *have made* a certain judgement, Baker and Morris sin against the prin-ciple, which they rightly accept, that *conscientia* is essentially present-tensed.

While it is important to distinguish between the perceptual and judgemental element in sensation as conceived by Descartes, the relation between the two, it must be admitted, is a complicated one. Let us consider a case in which the distinction between thought and judgement is particularly clear, namely the case of pain (itself one form of thought). In the *Principles* Descartes says:

> When a severe pain is felt, the perception of this pain may be very clear, and yet for all that not distinct, because it is usually confused by the sufferers with the obscure judgement that they form upon its nature, assuming as they do that something exists in the part affected, similar to the sensation of pain of which they are alone clearly conscious. (AT viii. 22: CSM i. 208)

Here Descartes clearly distinguishes the perception of pain and the judgement about pain. If the only elements involved in sensation were the bodily mechanism and the mental judgement, we would be in our bodies only as sailors in a ship; pain would be nothing more than an intellectual judgement about bodily damage. This, of course, is expressly denied in the Sixth Meditation (AT vii. 81; CSM ii. 56).

The judgement in question is, like all judgements of existence, a judgement about something extramental: namely, the condition of the part of the body in which the pain is felt. This judgement may be erroneous but the perception of pain cannot be in error. It is a childish mistake, according to Descartes, to think that pain is something outside our mind or perception. With pain, emotions, and appetites, as with the senses, we have to be on our guard not to judge about them anything beyond what is contained in our perception and inmost consciousness (*Principles*, part I, art. 66, AT viii. 32: CSM i. 216). In so far as pain is a thought, it is not located. We feel pain not in our members, but *as though* it were in our members. It is the judgement which we make about pain which locates it in a part of the body: this is a judgement which—unlike the pain itself—may be mistaken, as when a sufferer judges that the pain is in a limb which has in fact been amputated (cf. *Principles*, part IV, art. 196, AT viii. 320; CSM i. 283).

However, it is possible to have a clear and distinct perception of pain, provided that we regard it as nothing more than a sensation or thought (*Principles*, part I, art. 68, AT viii. 33: CSM i. 217). Now a clear and distinct perception forces the will to make a judgement, as Descartes makes clear in the Fourth Meditation. Citing the example of the Cogito he says 'I could not refrain from judging that what I so clearly understood was true...because from a great light in my intellect there followed an inclination of will' (AT vii. 59; CSM ii. 41; cf. also the Second Replies, AT vii. 166; CSM ii. 117). Will it not follow, therefore, that from a severe pain—or any other sensation—clearly perceived there will inevitably follow a judgement about that sensation? And will not this mean that the distinction between perception and judgement is vacuous for practical purposes?

The answer is to be found by distinguishing between clear perception and distinct perception. A perception can be clear without being distinct. Anyone who has a severe pain has a clear perception of it; but only a Cartesian initiate, who has followed the Meditations to the end of the Sixth, has a distinct perception of it (*Principles*, part I, art. 46, AT viii. 22: CSM i. 208). You can have a sensation without clearly and distinctly perceiving it; it is only if you realize that a sensation is strictly speaking no more than a thought that you perceive it distinctly. In the course of Cartesian purification the obscure judgement that pain is in my body is succeeded by the enlightened judgement that pain exists nowhere outside the mind. In each case the judgement is not about the content of the perception; it is about the relation of that perception to the extramental world. Only, in the first case it is a positive judgement and in the second a negative judgement.

Throughout our lives, ever since infancy in the womb, we have been having sensations which, according to Descartes, are thoughts belonging only to our minds. But as long as we are children, or Aristotelians, indeed as long as we have not yet read and absorbed the *Meditations*, we do not realize that that is what our sensations are. So we do not have the clear and distinct perception of them which forces a judgement about them. Only after the Sixth Meditation do we enjoy that great light in the intellect which produces the overpowering inclination of the will. Under the tuition of Descartes the voluntary and erroneous judgements of pre-Cartesian prejudice are replaced first, temporarily, by the suspension of judgement appropriate to Cartesian scepticism, and finally by the irresistible infallible judgements of Cartesian enlightenment.

If we leave aside the period when, once in a lifetime, we are calling our judgements into doubt, we can say that whenever we use our senses three things happen simultaneously. There is

the mechanical function in the body, there is the mental perception in the mind, and there is the judgement (erroneous or accurate) in the will. This is the threefold operation which is described
in the Sixth Replies, and it is this which, in Descartes's view, is the
true state of affairs masked by the confused Aristotelian conception of sensation from which we started. When Descartes uses
sentire to refer to the entire three-level process we may say that
this is a fifth sense of the word (E), corresponding to (B) + (C) +
(D) as identified above.

Sensations in senses (B) and (C) clearly are episodes in the
mind; sensations in sense (D) are events in the body. To what
does sensation in sense (E) belong? There is a famous letter to
Princess Elizabeth in which Descartes gives a list of primitive
notions.

> There are very few such notions. First, there are the most general—those
> of being, number, duration etc.—which apply to everything we can
> conceive. Then, as regards body in particular, we have only the notion
> of extension, which entails the notions of shape and motion; and as
> regards the soul on its own, we have only the notion of thought, which
> includes the perceptions of the intellect and the inclinations of the will.
> Lastly, as regards the soul and the body together, we have only the notion
> of their union, on which depends our notion of the soul's power to move
> the body, and the body's power to act on the soul and call its sensations
> and passions. (AT iii. 665: CSMK 218)

Some commentators have argued from this and kindred passages
that sensation is a mode not of mind nor of body, but of a third
entity, the complex human being: in these texts, they have
claimed, Descartes is not so much a dualist as a trialist, for he is
recognizing not just two but three fundamental categories of
substance.[4]

Trialism of this kind is one of the targets of Marlene Rosemond's marvellously erudite, patient, and insightful book. It is

---

[4] The term 'Cartesian trialism' appears to have been coined by J. Cottingham in
his article of the same name (*Mind*, 1985); cf. his *Descartes* (Oxford: Blackwell,
1986), 127 ff. On Cottingham's view, however, Descartes's third category is to be
construed attributively rather than substantively, i.e. as referring to the irreducib-
ility of psychophysical attributes such as sensation to modes of thought or extension. Martial Gueroult is an example of a commentator who interprets Descartes's
talk of the mind–body union substantivally, as referring to a substance psycho-
physique (*Descartes selon l'ordre des raisons*, 2nd edn., Montaigne: Paris, 1968), ii.
123–218.

in her sixth chapter that she examines sensation and its implications for dualism. Descartes is no trialist, she says: he never calls the human being a substance, and passages such as those quoted above do not involve any departure from dualism.

For Descartes sensations do constitute a new type of mode, which results from the union of body and soul; but they are not a third type of mode in addition to modes of thought and modes of extension: rather, they constitute a special subspecies of thought and they are modes of the mind, not of both mind and body or mind-body union. (DDR 173)

This seems to me correct in respect of sensation in sense (B), which is the sense in which Descartes is using the word in the final sentence of the passage quoted. On the other hand a statement of sensation in sense (E) records the occurrence of two modes, one of mind and one of body. But it is perfectly true that this involves no departure from dualism.

Rozemond, however, while rejecting trialism, also opposes what she calls 'interactionism', namely the standard interpretation according to which the union of body and soul in Descartes consists in the causal relationships between the two. She takes the passage in the letter to Elizabeth as implying 'that there is more to the union than just the fact of interaction . . . a grasp of interaction requires a grasp of the union and something about the union affords insight into interaction. And so the union plays a role in explaining mind-body interaction' (DDR 176).

I believe this to be a misunderstanding of the structure of this part of the letter. The union is related to the action of soul on body, and the action of body and soul, in the same way as thought is related to perception and volition. But thought is not an *explanation* of perception and volition; rather, it is the genus of which they are species. Similarly, union does not explain interaction; rather, soul-on-body causation and body-on-soul causation are the two species of interaction of which 'union' names the genus.

Rozemond seeks support for her thesis by appealing to the familiar passage of the Sixth Meditations where Descartes distinguished between his feelings of hunger, thirst, and pain and the purely intellectual awareness of bodily needs and injuries which he would have if he resided in his body only in the way that a sailor travels in his ship (AT vii. 81; CSM ii. 56). The sensations, he says, are confused modes of thinking that arise from the union and, as it were, intermingling of the mind with the body. This, according to Rozemond, shows that he thinks of the union as explaining 'the qualitative nature' of sensation.

The sense of this expression is not clear; no doubt it is an allusion to late twentieth-century philosophical talk of 'qualia' and the like. But while I agree with Rozemond that Descartes is an ancestor of such notions, I do not think that they assist in the understanding of the Sixth Meditation. The 'qualitative nature' of a sensation is presumably meant to be the kind of thing that makes the difference between the taste of cheese and the sound of a bassoon. But in the 'sailor in the ship' passage Descartes is not thinking of the difference between one sensation and another, but the difference between feeling and knowing, between sense and intellect. The same is true of the passage in the letter to Regius of January 1642 in which he says that an angel in a human body would not have sensation but simply perception of motion (AT iii. 493; CSMK 206).

Descartes does not discuss what *constitutes* the difference between sensations of different kinds: most likely he thought of it as something ineffable of which we are immediately aware. He does, often, discuss what *causes* the difference between sensations; but always in terms of the difference between their bodily causes. As he says, later in the same Meditation, 'a given motion in the brain must always produce the same sensation in the mind' (AT vii. 89: CSM ii. 61). Accordingly, I believe that the interactionist interpretation is the one which does most justice to Descartes's text. The 'intermingling' of mind and body is simply the reciprocal causation between the two.

Rosemond's own positive thesis about the ontological status of sensations (the thoughts which are sensations in sense (B) of 'sense') is that they are modes of the mind in so far as it united to the body. She has no difficulty in amassing familiar texts to show that Descartes regarded sensations as modes of the mind. The only problem here concerns the relation between sense and intellect. In the Sixth Replies passage Descartes urges us to distinguish carefully between sensation and intellection (AT vii. 437; CSM ii. 295). On the other hand in the *Principles* (part I, art. 32, AT VIII. 18; CSM i. 204) he says that sensation is a mode of perception, and perception is the operation of the intellect. The problem is not a serious one: all we need to do is to distinguish between senses of *intellectus* as we have distinguished between senses of *sensus*. There is a broad sense in which all cognitive, as opposed to volitional, activities of the mind are acts of intellect; there is a narrow sense, which Descartes sometimes calls 'pure intellection', in which intellect is distinguished from imagination and sense.

In a letter to Gibieuf, Descartes says that imagination and sense belong to the soul only in so far as it is joined to a body 'because they are kinds of thoughts without which one can conceive the soul in all its purity' (AT iii. 479: CSMK 203). Rozemond sees this, and a partially parallel passage in a letter to Regius (AT iii. 493: CSMK 2060), as leading to the following conclusion: 'Descartes sees the mind as a thinking thing, part of whose capacity for thought can be actualised in separation from the body, but part of which requires its union with the body' (DDR 189). This conclusion seems correct: but I wish to raise a further question. Is the dependence of sensation and imagination on the body a necessary or contingent dependence? Rozemond does not devote attention to this question. However, her discussion of the nature of sensation is read most naturally if the dependence on the body is taken as a necessary one: it is somehow logically impossible for sensation to occur in a mind that is not attached to a body.

In my own view, the link is contingent. Sensation in sense (E), of course, involves the body, for that sense was identified as being the use of *sentire* to refer to the concurrent operation of thought and motion. But sensation in the strict sense, sense (B), can, I believe, be conceived as taking place in a soul unattached to a body.

First of all, it is clear that the connections between sensations and bodily movements as they actually occur in a normal human body are contingent connections which can easily be altered. There is a particular motion in the brain which makes the mind feel a pain in the foot: but 'God could have made the nature of man such that this particular motion in the brain indicated something else to the mind; it might, for example, have made the mind aware of the actual motion occurring in the brain' (Sixth Meditation, AT vii. 88: CSM ii. 60). Equally, the feeling of pain in the foot might have been caused by some quite different motion in the brain. Still, it might be argued, even if any particular sensation–motion link is contingent, it is a necessary truth that there has to be some motion linked to a thought if that thought is to count as a sensation at all.

But we know that Descartes believed that wherever we can clearly and distinctly conceive of A without B, then it is possible at least by divine power for A to exist without B. As he says in the Sixth Meditation:

Because on the one hand I have a clear and distinct idea of myself inasmuch as I am only a thinking and unextended thing, and as, on the other, I possess a distinct idea of body, inasmuch as it is only an extended and unthinking thing, it is certain that this I is entirely and absolutely distinct from my body, and can exist without it. (AT vii. 78; CSM ii. 54)

The I which is clearly and distinctly conceived as a thinking thing which can exist without a body is the I of the Second Meditation, whose thoughts include a number of sensations. Therefore, it is possible at least by divine power for such sensations to occur without a body to cause them.

Indeed, the more clearly and distinctly we perceive the sensations, the more we detach them from their bodily causes. 'Pain and colour and so on are clearly and distinctly perceived when they are regarded merely as sensations or thoughts' (*Principles*, part I, art. 68, AT viii. 33: CSM i. 217). When we perceive them as arising from the mind's union of the body our perception of them is, by contrast, obscure. As Descartes wrote to Regius, 'we perceive that sensations of pain and all other sensations are not pure thoughts of a mind distinct from a body, but confused perceptions of a mind really united to one' (AT iii. 493: CSMK 206). We may be puzzled by this. The perceptions of a mature Cartesian, who has worked his way through the *Principles*, surely are not any longer confused. But then we look at the context, and we see that Descartes is instructing Regius on how to explain the union of body and soul to non-Cartesians.

As a matter of actual fact, sensations are, through the benevolent but unconstrained decrees of God, linked to bodily motions. But this is a matter of contingent providence, not of conceptual necessity. As children, or as adult Aristotelians, we are tempted to make the false judgement that sensations actually belong to the extramental world; but thanks to Descartes's endeavours, we can resist this temptation. What frees us from the temptation is precisely the realization of the contingency of the connection between mind and body, including the contingency of the connection between sensation and motion. God could, in his absolute omnipotence, have created beings which had all the sensations we have (taking 'sensation' in its strict sense) but who had no bodies.

In this essay I have been defending, against recent criticism, the traditional interpretation of Descartes as an interactionist dualist. I have not in any way been defending Descartes's dualism itself as a sound philosophical thesis. On the contrary I regard dualism as fundamentally and damagingly incoherent. But that is a different issue, on which I have written elsewhere. Here I have been concerned only with the content of Descartes's teaching, not with its philosophical merits.

III

Some Twentieth-Century Developments

9

The Thomism of Pope John Paul II: The Encyclical Letter *Fides et Ratio*

John Paul II is the most professional philosopher ever to occupy the papal throne. John XXI, who became Pope in 1276, two years after St Thomas Aquinas died, was long believed to be the Peter of Spain who wrote a popular logic textbook. But in the thirteenth century Spain produced more than one Peter and scholars now believe that the logician and the Pope were two different people. Pius X, when Bishop of Mantova, sacked the philosopher in his seminary and installed himself briefly as professor in his place. But no Pope has a record to compare with that of Karol Wojtyla, a full-time university professor of ethics in his thirties, with a series of academic publications to his name.

It is not surprising, then, that we now have a major encyclical devoted to the evaluation of philosophy and its relationship to the Catholic faith. Nor is it unprecedented: Leo XIII in his 1879 letter *Aeterni Patris*, much cited in the present letter, discussed the nature of philosophy and held up the teaching of Aquinas as a model to philosophers.

In the heyday of the Soviet Union, when it was difficult to detect shifts of power within the Communist Party, Kremlinologists would study carefully official photographs of the Central Committee. The information they sought was not to be found in the current array of stern unsmiling portraits: only comparison with previous photographs would reveal who was in, who was out, who had vanished altogether from the frame, and who had moved nearer the centre of the picture. So it is with papal documents. On superficial reading encyclicals, with their frequent obeisances to previous pontifical pronouncements, appear to be fundamentally a repetition of positions long held and frequently restated. But comparison with earlier documents often reveals significant, if silent, shifts of position.

Fides et Ratio differs in style and tone from the philosophical interventions of the Pope's predecessors. Historically, the Popes have contributed to philosophy principally by condemning propositions they did not like. John XXI, whether or not he was a philosopher by trade, was sufficiently interested in philosophy to instruct the Bishop of Paris to discipline the Aristotelians of his university. The upshot, in 1277, was a condemnation of 219 propositions, a victory for philosophical conservatism, and a defeat for those who, like Aquinas, had done their best to synthesize Christian doctrine with Aristotelian philosophy. Two centuries later, the learned nepotist Sixtus IV condemned a new-fangled three-valued logic taught at the young University of Louvain. In the nineteenth century Gregory XVI and Pius IX denounced, at regular intervals, individual idealists, fideists, and rationalists in France and Germany. Leo XIII himself in 1887 condemned forty propositions drawn from the works of the saintly Tyrolese philosopher, Antonio Rosmini.

It is all very different in *Fides et Ratio*. The Pope makes clear his dislike for philosophies of many different kinds; but no one is anathematized by name, no one's writings are declared offensive to pious ears. Philosophers of recent times are praised for their penetrating analyses of perception and experience, of the imaginary and the unconscious, of personhood and intersubjectivity, of freedom and values, of time and history. A few nineteenth-century thinkers are praised for 'courageous research': one of those thus singled out is none other than Antonio Rosmini. The philosopher pope more than once insists that the Church has no official philosophy and does not canonize any particular system in preference to others.

An encyclical is, by definition, a letter to bishops; and the effect it has depends above all on its impact on bishops in their dioceses. For bishops the Pope has a clear and simple message: restore philosophy to a place of honour in the training of the clergy. 'The study of philosophy is fundamental and indispensable', he says, 'to the formation of candidates for the priesthood'. Philosophy has been downgraded in Church circles, and this, in the Pope's opinion, has had a disastrous effect on Catholic theology. It will be interesting to see what reforms, as a result of *Fides et Ratio*, are introduced into the syllabus of the seminaries.

The Pope's letter, however, is addressed not only to bishops, but to theologians, philosophers, and all searchers after truth. For the theologians he has the warning that if they lack philosophical competence they will be 'swayed uncritically by assertions which have become part of current parlance and culture but which are poorly grounded in reason'. Those who refuse to learn from philosophy find themselves philosophizing unwittingly and badly.

What is the Pope's message for philosophers? Since he is addressing also 'those who are searching' he must intend his words to be read not only by Christians, but also by members of other faiths and those who are agnostic. What will philosophers outside the Pope's domain make of *Fides et Ratio*?

They will no doubt heartily agree that if theologians were better versed in philosophy they might not write so much trendy waffle. But they will wish to know exactly what the Pope means by 'philosophy'. He thinks of a philosophy as being an organized system of knowledge; but he tells us that 'every philosophical system, while it should always be respected in its wholeness, without any instrumentalization, must still recognize the primacy of philosophical enquiry'. A privileged position is, however, given to that 'classical philosophy' whose terms have been used for the formulation of Catholic dogma. The Pope believes that there is a universal philosophy which includes knowledge of the principles of non-contradiction, causality, and finality. One cannot help wondering what version of 'the principle of finality' would be accepted in common by, say, Aristotle, Augustine, Descartes, and Kant. But the Pope tells us that this philosophy is an implicit possession of all mankind. Its principal task is 'to ask the question of life's meaning and to sketch an answer to it'.

Much of *Fides et Ratio* is a non-controversial narrative of the relationship between Catholic Christianity and philosophy as so understood. Historians will note some interesting omissions and inclusions in the Pope's list of his favourite Christian philosophers. Augustine, naturally, figures prominently; not quite so predictably, he is paired with Gregory Nazianzen. Of the medieval philosophers, St Anselm, St Bonaventure and St Thomas Aquinas are singled out as the 'great triad'. Aquinas' presence on the list can be taken for granted, and in this eirenic letter it is unsurprising to see the gentle and imaginative Anselm preferred to the rumbustious encyclopaedic Albert. Again, one can understand why the irregular Abelard and the schismatic Ockham do not appear on the pontifical list. From a philosophical point of view, however, Bonaventure should surely have been trumped by his recently beatified fellow Franciscan, John Duns Scotus, subtlest of all the scholastics.

Only two philosophers are mentioned between the thirteenth and the nineteenth century; one is Suarez and the other is Pascal. Then in the nineteenth century we are given Newman and Rosmini and the Russians Chaadev and Soloviev, and in the twentieth Maritain, Gilson, and Edith Stein from the West, plus Florensky and Lossky from Russia. Kierkegaard is the only Protestant to be mentioned.

Modern philosophy between Descartes and Kant is passed over in silence. 'Abandoning the investigation of being', the Pope says, 'modern philosophical research has concentrated instead upon human knowing'. Descartes is not mentioned by name; but already in his book *The Acting Person* (1969) Cardinal Wojtyla had set himself the task of reversing the Cartesian identification of human personality with self-consciousness.

John Paul is, of course, far from being the only contemporary philosopher to believe that Descartes set philosophy on a disastrous course. When, in his sixth chapter, the Pope turns to denounce contemporary errors, he will not lack allies among secular philosophers. Many will join him in denouncing nihilism (if that means a negation of objective truth) and pragmatism (if that means a total abandonment of ethical principles). Like Frege, the Pope attacks historicism, insisting that a truth remains a truth for all time. Like Wittgenstein, he attacks the scientism which assimilates all human thought to the mode of operation of the natural sciences. Only the attack on 'eclecticism' seems to miss its mark. To be sure, if eclecticism is simply the use of jargon torn from its context, it deserves the Pope's rebuke: but if it is the attempt to combine the best elements of different philosophical traditions, what is wrong with it? After all, *The Acting Person* aimed to combine the insights of Aquinas with those of Max Scheler. And is not *Fides et Ratio* itself a highly eclectic document?

Secular philosophers will have problems, however, when the Pope says that it is a function of philosophy to serve the propagation of the Gospel. Bertrand Russell once claimed that a Christian philosopher cannot have the true philosophical spirit: he cannot, like Socrates, follow an argument wherever it may lead, since he knows the truth in advance, all declared in the Catholic faith. Is this charge justified by the teaching of *Fides et Ratio*?

The letter more than once affirms the autonomy of philosophy. It operates by reason, not by faith; it has its own methods and its own principles. It must not bend its own rules in order to reach edifying conclusions. 'Otherwise there would be no guarantee that it would remain oriented to truth and that it was moving towards truth by way of a process governed by reason.' Philosophy used to be called *ancilla theologiae*, the maidservant of theology, but the Pope tells us that this is no longer an appropriate description of philosophy. How then can he say that the vocation of philosophy is 'to offer its rational and critical resources that theology, as the understanding of faith, may be fruitful and creative'?

It is not easy to reconcile the claim that philosophy is autonomous with two others of the Pope's theses: that the task of philosophy is to discover the meaning of life, and that the meaning of life is something settled once for all by Christianity. If these three theses are all true, then philosophy's task is already done before it begins. Philosophy can only be genuinely autonomous if it is free to reach the conclusion that life has a meaning quite different from that given it by Christianity, or even that 'the meaning of life' is a phrase with no clear meaning. Of course, the Pope believes that anyone who reaches such a conclusion must have gone wrong in his philosophy; but that is something he believes as a matter of faith, not something he knows as a philosopher. Even the Pope's own philosophy is not above the law of theology.

In response to *Fides et Ratio* it seems that we must distinguish between two kinds of autonomy: an autonomy of method, and an autonomy of result.

The Pope recognizes that philosophy enjoys an autonomy of method. The processes of faith and reason are quite distinct, in the sense that the premises of philosophical argument are very different from those of theological argument. The philosopher may not appeal, as the theologian may, to any specific divine revelation. He may not argue from scripture, or tradition, or the experience of the saints. All he can put forward are facts of observation or straightforward truths of reason. In this sense, the philosopher is independent of the theologian.

But does the Pope accept the autonomy of philosophy in respect of the results it may reach? Suppose that a philosopher, following the argument where it leads, comes to a conclusion which is at variance with Catholic dogma. Does the autonomy of philosophy mean that the Church should respect this conclusion? No: it must exercise, the Pope tells us 'critical discernment of opinions and philosophies which contradict Christian doctrine'. Philosophy enjoys autonomy with regard to premisses, but not with regard to conclusions. Its freedom is not the freedom to journey to different destinations, but freedom to reach the one possible destination by different routes.

Many times in his encyclical the Pope invites us to attend to the philosophy of St Thomas. There is no doubt that, judged even by purely secular standards, Aquinas is a most remarkable philosopher. Russell was wrong to say that he could not be a true philosopher because as a Christian he was seeking for reasons for what he already believed. 'The finding of arguments for a conclusion given in advance', Russell complained, 'is not philosophy, but special pleading.' It has often been observed that this remark came oddly from a philosopher who in *Principia Mathematica* took hundreds of pages to prove that one and one make two. We judge a philosopher by whether his reasonings are sound or unsound; not by where he first lighted on his premisses or how he came to believe his conclusions. Judged by the acuteness of his intellect and the breadth of his vision, Aquinas fully deserves his place in the philosophical pantheon with Plato and Aristotle, Descartes and Kant.

During the Middle Ages Aquinas did not enjoy any unique position of respect among Catholic philosophers. It was only after Leo XIII's encyclical that he came to be regarded as the official philosopher of the Catholic Church; a position reinforced when Pius X singled out twenty-four theses of Thomist philosophy to be taught in Catholic institutions.

This apotheosis of Thomism did harm as well as good to Aquinas's reputation as a philosopher. It caused many secular philosophers to dismiss him as simply a spokesman for Catholicism. It meant too that his opinions and arguments were frequently presented in crude ways by philosophically unskilled admirers. On the other hand, many serious scholars were inspired by Leo's encyclical to place the learned world in their debt for their work as editors or interpreters of the saint.

The revival of Thomism, whatever its philosophical merits, was highly significant in theology. As John Paul says 'the most influential Catholic theologians of the present century, to whose thinking and research the Second Vatican Council was much indebted, were the products of this revival of Thomistic philosophy'. It is remarkable, therefore, that one of the results of the Second Vatican Council was a downgrading of Aquinas's importance. In recent years he has lost much of his ecclesiastical pre-eminence, and his works have been superseded, in the reading lists of ordinands, by fashionable writings judged more relevant to the contemporary scene.

The irony of this is not lost on the Pope. He laments that in the years since the Council a sense of the importance of philosophy has been diminished, so that it is now necessary 'to reiterate the value of the Angelic Doctor's insights and insist on the study of his thought'.

There is a second paradox. In non-Catholic circles the wind of ecclesiastical change blew no harm to Aquinas's reputation. Philosophers who had ignored him as a propagandist for Catholicism began to value him as a philosopher in his own right. A shining example of the secular Thomist revival was Professor Norman Kretzmann of Cornell, who died in 1998, never having been a Catholic and having been for much of his life an atheist. Seven years previously Kretzmann was told that he had terminal cancer. He devoted those last years of his life to writing a magisterial three-volume commentary on the *Summa contra Gentiles*.

The Aquinas whom the Pope holds up as a model is a less pugnacious philosopher than the hero of *Aeterni Patris*. According to Leo 'he refuted by himself the errors of preceding times, and has provided invincible weapons for the refutation of errors that were to be ever springing up in days to come'. John Paul, on the other hand, commends him for 'undertaking a dialogue with the Arab and Jewish thinkers of his time'. He tells us that when the magisterium has held up Thomas as a model 'this has not been in order to take a position on properly philosophical questions nor to demand adherence to particular theses'. We have come some distance from Pius X.

Though he may be a model of philosophical method, Aquinas cannot be cited to prove the beneficent effects of ecclesiastical intervention in philosophical issues. If he had obeyed the Papal Legate to the University of Paris who banned Aristotle's metaphysics and physics in 1215, Aquinas would never have written some of his most valuable works. If he had survived to undergo the episcopal condemnation of 1277 he would have had to tear up some of his most interesting writings. Aquinas was a great philosopher in spite of, not because of, the ecclesiastical constraints under which he worked.

Of course, St Thomas drew much of his philosophical, as well as theological, inspiration, from his meditation on the Bible and on the writings of the Christian Fathers: but reverence to sacred texts and loyalty to religious traditions is something different from subjection to an intrusive magisterium.

Philosophers will be grateful for the compliment which *Fides et Ratio* pays to their profession; but they will find it difficult to reciprocate wholeheartedly the papal embrace. An encyclical is, after all, not an ideal medium for the communication of a philosophical message. Poised halfway between the anathemas of old and the *Analecta Husserliana* of today, it lacks the sharp clarity of the first and the scholarly sophistication of the second. Perhaps it is unsurprising that there have hitherto been no philosopher popes: the two professions must be very difficult to combine.

10

The Stylometric Study
of the Aristotelian Writings

In recent years A. Q. Morton, A. D. Winspear, and S. Michaelson have applied stylometric techniques to a number of works of Aristotle with a view to settling long-standing scholarly questions about the genuineness and composition of certain disputed texts. (See, in particular, 'The Nicomachean Ethics of Aristotle', in *It's Greek to the Computer* by Morton and Winspear (1971); and 'The Authorship and Integrity of the Athenaion Politeia' by Morton and Michaelson in *Proceedings of the Royal Society of Edinburgh*, 1971–2). The technique used has been to select a stylistic feature (e.g. sentence-length, or the occurrence of frequent words such as conjunctions and introductory particles) and to study it both in the disputed text in question and in two or three texts taken as definitively Aristotelian—texts such as the *Parts of Animals*, the *De Interpretatione*, the *De Caelo*, or the *De Anima*, the authorship of which can be regarded as a defining characteristic of the Aristotle of tradition. When statistically significant differences in respect of the distribution of these features are detected between the disputed texts and the paradigmatic Aristotelian texts, this is taken in the absence of any obvious alternative explanation as evidence that the disputed texts are un-Aristotelian. Thus, for instance, when it is found that the differences between the second half of the *Ath. Pol.* on the one hand, and the *De Anima and De Interpretatione* on the other, in respect of the use of ἀλλά, γάρ, μέν, δέ and καί at the beginning of sentences, are so large that *Ath. Pol.* B is most unlikely to be a sample from the same population, this is taken as confirming that *Ath. Pol.* B is very unlikely to be a work of Aristotle. The conclusion is drawn from a number of such tests, independent of each other, 'That not only is *Ath. Pol.* not a work of Aristotle but that it is so unlike his work that it is difficult to see how the suggestion that it might be Aristotelian would ever have gained support had it not been early assumed.' (*PRSE* (1971–2), 94)

The study of the *Athenaion Politeia* is one of the most impressive products of what Morton calls 'The New Stylometry', and many Aristotelian scholars would be predisposed on other grounds to accept its conclusions. None the less a question concerning the method used must have occurred to many readers of the paper. How justified are we in drawing conclusions from a comparison between the *Ath. Pol.* and such a small number of Aristotle's works (namely, the *De Anima, Parts of Animals, Progression of Animals, De Interpretatione, and Politics)?* Can it be assumed in advance that Aristotle was consistent in the speech habits which these tests measured? If he was not consistent, or consistent only to a small degree, then the differences between the paradigms and the *Ath. Pol.* prove nothing; on the other hand, even if he was, in the great majority of his writing, consistent in these habits, can we be sure that in the *De Interpretatione* and the *De Anima*—for instance—we have chosen representative texts?

Morton and Michaelson no doubt felt justified in assuming that Aristotle was consistent in these habits because of their studies of other authors, especially the Greek orators and the New Testament writers, which showed a considerable degree of such consistency in those writers. None the less, it seemed to me that it would be interesting, both for its own sake and as providing to a certain extent a check on stylometric methods of this type, to investigate the whole of Aristotle's writings by similar methods to discover whether that corpus does reveal the hand of a single author consistent in the relevant speech habits. In order to provide a further test of the method, and to apply it so far as possible in independence of the subjective conclusions of scholars, it seemed desirable to apply the tests to the whole corpus as handed down in the MSS, and not to restrict them to those works commonly accepted as genuine: not with any initial assumption that the works generally regarded as spurious in fact have any claim to be genuine, but with the expectation that if the stylometric methods are generally valid the spuriousness of the spurious works will reveal itself *ambulando* in the application of the tests.

The present essay reports the results of the applications of two tests, based on Morton's work, to the Aristotelian corpus. In the

Stylometric Study of Aristotelian Writings 129

studies of the *Nicomachean Ethics* and the *Athenaion Politeia* use is made of the proportion of sentences which contain δέ as their second or third word as an indicator of authorship. There and elsewhere Morton has suggested that the occurrence of γάρ as the second or third word of a sentence may also be characteristic. The test to be described in the first part of what follows is a combination of these two tests. In the *Ath. Pol.* paper use is also made of a comparison of the last words of sentences, classified as nouns, verbs, or neither: the nature and rationale of this test is explained at length in the paper by Michaelson and Morton 'Last Words: A Test of Authorship for Greek Writers', *New Testament Studies*, 18 (1972), 192–208. This test was applied to the whole Aristotelian corpus with the results described in part II of the present paper. A comparison and combination of the results of these two tests is given in the third and final part.

I am indebted for advice and assistance in understanding the tests to be applied and for comments on an earlier draft of this paper, to the Rev A. Q. Morton; and for assistance in counting and in interpreting the results of counting to Messrs Jonathan Barnes, R. Binkley, N. Denyer, the Rev H. Wren, and Frl. U. Wolf. All counting was done manually; the computer was used only for the statistical analysis of the results.

I

A sample was taken from each of 123 books in the Aristotelian corpus. (Of all the works, genuine and spurious, occurring in Bekker's edition only the *Problems* was omitted, because of the special difficulties presented by its question-and-answer form.) The samples normally consisted of the first one hundred sentences of the book; in the case of some smaller works (e.g. in the *Parva Naturalia*) a sample of fifty sentences was used, or else the whole work was counted. Partly to provide a check on the adequacy of this method of sampling, a number of works (each book of the *Topics*, *Met* EZHΛMN, *EN* 6, 7, *EE* II) were used as samples in their entirety.

In each sample the sentences were classified into three groups: those containing δέ as second or third word, those containing γάρ as second or third word, and those containing neither as second or third word. Since no normal sentence contains both δέ and γάρ in its second and third words, the three groups were mutually exclusive and exhaustive. The classification and counting of sentences was done entirely by hand, so that it is to be assumed that the results incorporate the customary amount of human error. For all samples the text of Bekker's edition was used: this was in order to reduce so far as possible the effects of editorial decisions by different hands. Following Wake and Morton, a sentence was defined as a group of words ending with a full stop (.), a colon, (·), or an interrogation mark (;). The use of this definition is claimed to have the effect of minimizing differences between texts from different editors.

The results of the counting were tested for statistical significance in the following manner. First, each sample was split into two or more sections—in the standard case, the hundred sentence sample was split into two sections, sentences 1–50 and sentences 51–100—and these sections were subjected to a chi-squared test to see whether the differences between them were such as were to be expected from two samples from a homogeneous population. After the internal consistency of the sample had been tested in this manner the results of the different samples making up a single work—e.g. the eight one-hundred sentence samples from the books of the *Physics*—were placed in a contingency table and given a chi-squared test for statistical significance. Finally, a large block of samples from works of different kinds was built up: it contained the samples from each book of the *Analytics*, each book of the Physics except VII, each book of the *De Caelo*, *De Generatione et Corruptione*, *Meterologica*, the *Parva Naturalia*, the *De Motu Animalium*, books ΑΓΒΔΘΙ of the *Metaphysics*, books 2–7 of the *Nicomachean Ethics*, each book of the *Politics*, and the *Poetics*. This constituted an internally consistent sample of 4,723 sentences. 1,693 of these (35.9%) had δέ at the beginning; 1,559 (33.0%) had γάρ; and 1,471 (31.1%) had neither. Each of the 123 samples was then tested against this block by a chi-squared test to ascertain whether it could be regarded as a sample from the same population as the block.

The results of the testing are presented in Tables 10.1 and 10.2. The first column of Table 10.1 lists the works sampled in the order in which they occur in Bekker's *Aristotle*. The second column records the consensus of scholars concerning the genuineness of the work. The consensus was ascertained in the following manner: Ross's *Aristotle*, Jaeger's *Aristotle*, Düring's article *Aristotles* in the vol. xi supplement of Pauly-Wissowa's *Realencyclopädie*, Kerferd's article *Aristotle* in Paul Edwards's *Encyclopedia of Philosophy*, and Gauthier's Introduction (2nd edn) to Gauthier-Jolif's *Ethique à Nicomaque* were consulted. Where these authors were unanimous about the genuineness or spuriousness of a work, it was recorded as genuine or spurious; if they disagreed, its status was recorded as doubtful.[1] The third column specifies the sample used. The next column records the number of sentences in the sample beginning with δέ, with γάρ or with neither. The penultimate column gives the internal chi-squared, for the appropriate degrees of freedom, obtained by testing the several portions of the sample against each other. The final column gives the fit between the sample in question and the large block. The chi-squared results in this column are all for two degrees of freedom, since testing the block as a single whole against the individual samples gives in each case a 3×2 contingency table. For two degrees of freedom, a result below 5.99 is not significant at the 5% level, a result between 5.99 and 9.21 is significant at the 5% level, and any result above 9.21 is significant at the 1% level.

Table 10.2 shows the degree of internal consistency of whole works. The second column lists the number of samples taken (this is the same as the number of books, if more than one, in the work in question). The totals of the different types of sentence from the samples of the work are next given, and then the chi-squared which results from testing the different samples all together is given, with the appropriate number of degrees of freedom. The final column shows the significance of the result, '0' indicating that no statistically significant difference is found between the samples, '5' that the differences between them were significant at the 5% level, and '1' that the differences were significant at the 1% level. In a number of cases in both tables 'N.A.' indicates that the chi-squared test was not applicable because the expected value in one of the cells of the contingency table was less than 5.

---

[1] As an Aristotelian scholar, I do not in all cases agree with the consensus of these authors: I use them as representatives of the scholarly tradition for purposes of comparison with the statistical results.

Table 10.1.

	Work	Consensus	Sample	δέ	γάρ	Neither	Int. Chi^2	Fit to Block
1	*Categories*	Doubtful	1–100	45	34	21	3.53 for 2	5.56
2	*De Interp*	Genuine	do.	46	23	31	1.62 for 2	6.99
3	*Anal Pr* I	Genuine	do.	40	31	29	2.58 for 2	0.74
4	*Anal Pr* II	Genuine	do.	32	37	31	1.22 for 2	0.88
5	*An Post* I	Genuine	do.	43	32	25	0.50 for 2	2.61
6	*An Post* II	Genuine	do.	33	26	41	1.14 for 2	4.72
7	*Topics* I	Genuine	whole	141	115	79	9.54 for 10	9.37
8	*Topics* II	Genuine	whole	111	115	88	6.87 for 10	2.10
9	*Topics* III	Genuine	whole	60	74	87	1.52 for 2	9.05
10	*Topics* IV	Genuine	whole	94	171	121	2.86 for 10	27.47
11	*Topics* V	Doubtful	whole	127	154	145	12.20 for 10	6.23
12	*Topics* VI	Genuine	whole	133	237	159	3.73 for 10	35.21
13	*Topics* VII	Genuine	whole	46	55	51	1.26 for 2	2.01
14	*Topics* VIII	Genuine	whole	150	131	89	12.91 for 10	0.85
15	*Soph El*	Genuine	1–100	41	30	29	0.55 for 2	1.14
16	*Physics* I	Genuine	do.	28	37	35	8.62 for 2	2.63
17	*Physics* II	Genuine	do.	32	35	33	3.00 for 2	0.63
18	*Physics* III	Genuine	do.	34	33	33	1.86 for 2	0.20
19	*Physics* IV	Genuine	do.	34	37	29	4.36 for 2	0.71
20	*Physics* V	Genuine	do.	31	34	35	1.24 for 2	1.14
21	*Physics* VI	Genuine	do.	36	33	31	0.20 for 2	0.00
22	*Physics* VII	Genuine	do.	22	40	38	11.24 for 2	8.19
23	*Physics* VIII	Genuine	do.	31	35	34	12.82 for 2	1.02
24	*De Cael* I	Genuine	do.	33	35	32	0.00 for 2	0.36
25	*De Cael* II	Genuine	do.	34	38	28	2.00 for 2	0.54
26	*De Cael* III	Genuine	do.	37	33	30	2.25 for 2	0.08
27	*De Cael* IV	Genuine	do.	44	32	24	1.16 for 2	3.45
28	*De C & C* I	Genuine	do.	33	28	39	7.10 for 2	2.90
29	*De C & C* II	Genuine	do.	37	34	29	1.36 for 2	0.21
30	*Meteor* I	Genuine	do.	35	32	33	0.24 for 2	0.16
31	*Meteor* II	Genuine	do.	39	33	28	2.74 for 2	0.38
32	*Meteor* III	Genuine	do.	41	31	28	0.88 for 2	1.16
33	*Meteor* IV	Doubtful	do.	43	27	30	0.82 for 2	1.24
34	*De Mundo*	Spurious	do.	43	7	50	N.A.	18.41
35	*De An* I	Genuine	1–200	112	56	32	0.79 for 2	36.68
36	*De An* II	Genuine	do.	102	57	41	5.11 for 2	23.93
37	*De An* III	Genuine	SS 1–100	39	28	33	0.40 for 2	2.77
38	*De S & S*	Genuine	101–200	36	28	36	0.00 for 2	0.63
39	*De M & R*	Genuine	1–50	15	15	20	0.03 for 2	1.85
40	*De S & V*	Genuine	1–50	19	16	15	0.79 for 2	0.10
41	*De Som*	Genuine	do.	15	16	19	0.36 for 2	1.23
42	*De D p S*	Genuine	do.	17	21	12	0.95 for 2	2.07
43	*De L & B*	Genuine	do.	14	18	18	3.18 for 2	1.36
44	*De V & M*	Genuine	do.	20	17	13	0.95 for 2	0.67
45	*De Resp*	Genuine	do.	19	15	16	0.19 for 2	0.21
46	*De Spir*	Spurious	do.	25	16	19	1.06 for 2	1.29
47	*Hist An* I	Doubtful	1–100	55	19	26	7.79 for 2	16.62
48	*Hist An* II	Doubtful	do.	69	19	12	0.82 for 2	47.01
49	*Hist An* III	Doubtful	do.	62	11	27	2.56 for 2	33.52

50	*Hist An* IV	Doubtful	do.	79	8	13	N.A.	78.97
51	*Hist An* V	Doubtful	do.	64	18	18	0.73 for 2	33.53
52	*Hist An* VI	Doubtful	do.	68	13	19	5.54 for 2	44.43
53	*Hist An* VII	Spurious	do.	46	21	33	1.48 for 2	7.22
54	*Hist An* VIII	Doubtful	do.	45	40	15	0.19 for 2	10.54
55	*Hist An* IX	Spurious	do.	46	37	17	1.76 for 2	9.62
56	*Hist An* X	Spurious	do.	47	17	36	1.13 for 2	11.80
57	*De P An* I	Genuine	do.	32	37	31	2.32 for 2	0.88
58	*De P An* II	Genuine	do.	38	34	28	1.82 for 2	0.47
59	*De P An* III	Genuine	1–300	152	99	49	0.95 for 2	41.52
60	*De P An* IV	Genuine	1–100	47	29	24	1.03 for 2	5.47
61	*De M An*	Genuine	do.	40	33	26	6.38 for 2	1.31
62	*De In An*	Genuine	do.	45	30	25	0.76 for 2	3.74
63	*De G An* I	Genuine	do.	47	33	20	0.06 for 2	4.66
64	*De G An* II	Genuine	do.	41	31	28	3.56 for 2	1.16
65	*De G An* III	Genuine	do.	40	34	26	2.35 for 2	1.33
66	*De C An* IV	Genuine	do.	47	27	26	9.83 for 2	5.29
67	*De G An* V	Genuine	do.	40	40	20	3.20 for 2	5.85
68	*De Color*	Spurious	1–100	38	37	25	0.16 for 2	1.79
69	*De Audib*	Spurious	do.	44	39	17	0.92 for 2	9.22
70	*Physiogn*	Spurious	do.	37	21	42	6.43 for 2	8.03
71	*De Plan* I	Spurious	do.	38	18	44	0.16 for 2	12.02
72	*De Plan* II	Spurious	do.	33	24	43	0.25 for 2	7.03
73	*De Mir Aus*	Spurious	do.	51	10	39	0.49 for 2	24.08
74	*Mechan*	Spurious	whole	31	32	39	3.04 for 2	2.52
75	*De Lin Ins*	Spurious	1–100	33	33	34	5.8 for 2	0.48
76	*Vent Sit*	Spurious	whole	26	6	18	N.A.	10.62
77	*De Meliss*	Spurious	1–100	27	34	39	4.01 for 2	4.11
78	*Metaph* A	Genuine	do.	28	33	39	5.88 for 2	3.62
79	*Metaph* α	Doubtful	whole	23	31	29	4.80 for 2	2.35
80	*Metaph* B	Genuine	1–100	30	34	36	2.01 for 2	1.70
81	*Metaph* Γ	Genuine	do.	39	24	37	1.32 for 2	3.77
82	*Metaph* Δ	Genuine	do.	37	24	39	2.00 for 2	4.39
83	*Metaph* E	Doubtful	whole	30	33	49	0.08 for 2	9.47
84	*Metaph* Z	Genuine	whole	206	199	247	4.42 for 2	12.15
85	*Metaph* H	Genuine	whole	70	36	74	7.30 for 2	14.60
86	*Metaph* Θ	Genuine	1–100	32	33	35	5.82 for 2	0.87
87	*Metaph* I	Genuine	do.	41	23	35	6.90 for 2	4.45
88	*Metaph* K	Doubtful	do.	36	39	25	0.82 for 2	2.25
89	*Metaph* Λ	Genuine	whole	110	103	161	17.36 for 14	21.23
90	*Metaph* M	Genuine	whole	154	158	189	23.60 for 20	8.31
91	*Metaph* N	Genuine	whole	76	69	129	15.22 for 10	29.84
92	*E Nic* I	Genuine	1–200	84	59	53	3.85 for 2	3.16
93	*E Nic* II	Genuine	1–100	36	34	30	1.64 for 2	0.07
94	*E Nic* III	Genuine	do.	37	29	34	1.94 for 2	0.77
95	*E Nic* IV	Genuine	do.	38	34	28	0.20 for 2	0.47
96	*E Nic* V	Genuine	do.	37	33	30	4.64 for 2	0.41
97	*E Nic* VI	Genuine	whole	72	79	113	4.16 for 10	16.61
98	*E Nic* VII	Genuine	whole	121	116	142	6.96 for 10	6.57
99	*E Nic* VIII	Genuine	1–100	41	37	22	0.04 for 2	3.84
100	*E Nic* IX	Genuine	do.	41	33	26	0.46 for 2	1.56
102	*M Mor* I	Doubtful	1–100	20	39	41	0.45 for 2	11.02
103	*M Mor* II	Doubtful	do.	31	38	31	0.44 for 2	1.38

Table 10.1. (*contd*)

	Work	Consensus	Sample	δέ	γάρ	Neither	Int. Chi^2	Fit to Block
104	*E Eud* I	Genuine	do.	33	34	33	2.72 for 2	0.36
105	*E Eud* II	Genuine	whole	149	98	175	10.54 for 10	5.56
106	*E Eud* III	Genuine	1–100	29	34	37	1.94 for 2	2.39
107	*E Eud* VII	Genuine	do.	36	31	33	0.08 for 2	0.23
108	*De V and V*	Spurious	whole	65	0	9	N.A.	92.17
109	*Pol* I	Genuine	1–100	38	33	29	5.42 for 2	0.27
110	*Pol* II	Genuine	do.	31	35	34	0.55 for 2	1.02
111	*Pol* III	Genuine	do.	26	35	39	0.44 for 2	4.71
112	*Pol* IV	Genuine	do.	35	33	32	2.17 for 2	0.04
113	*Pol* V	Genuine	do.	40	31	29	0.26 for 2	0.74
114	*Pol* VI	Genuine	do.	35	40	25	2.16 for 2	2.60
115	*Pol* VII	Genuine	do.	36	33	31	1.41 for 2	0.00
116	*Pol* VIII	Genuine	do.	33	38	29	4.25 for 2	1.10
117	*Econ* I	Spurious	do.	44	31	25	0.07 for 2	3.12
118	*Econ* II	Spurious	do.	61	4	35	N.A.	42.93
119	*Rhet* I	Genuine	do.	35	36	29	0.45 for 2	0.43
120	*Rhet* II	Genuine	do.	21	37	42	1.63 for 2	10.22
121	*Rhet* III	Genuine	do.	34	27	39	2.55 for 2	3.10
122	*Rh ad Al*	Spurious	1–50	19	12	19	N.A.	2.03
123	*Poet*	Genuine	1–100	39	30	31	0.4 for 2	0.54

Table 10.2.

Work	No samples	δέ	γάρ	Neither	Chi^2	Significance
Categories	2	45	34	21	3.53 for 2	0
De Interp	2	46	23	31	1.62 for 2	0
Prior Anal	2	72	68	60	1.48 for 2	0
Poster Anal	2	76	56	66	5.82 for 2	0
Topics	8	1,162	1,053	819	30.62 for 14	1
Soph Elench	2	41	30	29	0.55 for 2	0
Physics	8	248	284	268	7.00 for 14	0
De Caelo	4	148	138	114	3.84 for 6	0
De Gen & Corr	2	70	66	62	2.28 for 2	0
Meteorologica	4	115	125	119	2.47 for 6	0
De Mundo	2	62	7	31	N.A.	—
De Anima	3	144	84	71	6.77 for 4	0
Parva Naturalia	8	145	135	122	14.11 for 14	0
De Spiritu	2	25	16	19	1.06 for 2	0
De Hist An	10	580	203	217	99.84 for 18	1
De Part An	4	169	135	96	14.48 for 6	5
De Motu An	2	40	33	26	6.43 for 2	5
De Inc An	2	45	30	25	0.76 for 2	0
De Gen An	5	215	165	120	5.37 for 8	0
De Color	2	38	27	25	0.16 for 2	0
De Audib	2	44	39	17	0.92 for 2	0
Physiogn	2	37	21	42	6.43 for 2	5
De Plant	4	71	42	87	0.46 for 2	0

De Mirab Ausc	2	51	10	39	0.49 for 2	0
Mechanica	2	31	32	39	3.04 for 2	0
De Lin Insec	2	33	33	34	5.80 for 2	0
Vent Sit	2	26	6	18	N.A.	
Meliss Xen	2	27	34	39	4.01 for 2	0
Metaphysics	14	439	414	530	38.52 for 26	0
Nic Ethics	7	271	235	194	11.35 for 12	0
Disputed Books	3	93	94	113	5.08 for 4	0
Magna Moralia	2	51	77	72	3.77 for 2	0
Eudemian Ethics	4	128	127	145	3.23 for 6	0
De V and V	2	65	0	9	N.A.	
Politics	8	274	278	248	9.47 for 14	0
Economica	2	105	35	60	N.A.	
Rhetoric	3	90	100	110	8.41 for 4	0
Rhet ad Al	2	19	12	19	N.A.	
Poetics	2	39	30	31	0.4 for 2	0

The feature which emerges most strikingly from the results is that the use of δέ and γάρ does appear to be a characteristic in which the authors of the Aristotelian corpus are, within a local context, very consistent. The overwhelming majority of the samples taken proved on test to be internally consistent. Of the 123 samples listed in Table 10.1 only the following show internal differences significant at the 1% level: *Physics* VII, *Physics* VIII, *De Gen. An.* IV. The first of these is from a book with a highly anomalous textual history (cf. Ross, Aristotle's *Physics*). No such immediate explanation presents itself for the other two anomalous results, but it is perhaps not necessary to look for any other than chance. The books which were sampled as wholes, and divided into sections of 50 sentences (*Topics* I–II, IV–VI, VIII; *Met* ΛMN) show a high degree of internal consistency, and confirm the adequacy of 100-sentence samples as representatives of whole books.

The local consistency of the use of δέ and γάρ at the beginning of sentences does not of course indicate without further ado that it can be used as a test of authorship: it might on the one hand be an instantiation of a feature common to all writers of Greek prose, or on the other hand be variable within the writings of a single author over changes of time or subject-matter. The first of these hypotheses can be ruled out from within the Aristotelian corpus itself: the habits of the authors of the second book of the *Economica* and of the *De Virtutibus et Vitiis*, for instance, clearly differ from those displayed in the majority of the corpus. The

Table 10.3.

	Good fit to block	Diffs sign. at 5%	Diffs sign. at 1%
Genuine	71	5	13
Doubtful	5	1	9
Spurious	7	4	8

suggestion in the second hypothesis that the habit may vary with changes of subject-matter conflicts with the possibility of building up a large homogeneous block drawn from Aristotelian writings on logic, physics, biology, metaphysics, ethics, and politics. No light is cast on the hypothesis of change over time by the present results.

Table 10.3 shows the most important feature of the results so far as concerns the possibility of using the test as a test of authorship.

It will be seen that of the eighty-nine works in the corpus regarded as genuine by scholars, seventy-one (79.7%) when tested against the test block show no statistically significant differences in the distribution of δέ and γάρ at the beginning of sentences; but thirteen (14.6%) of the samples cannot be regarded as random samples from the same population as the test block. This shows immediately that the δέ–γάρ test cannot be used in any straightforward way as a decisive test of authorship. Among the thirteen works which would be rejected by the crude use of this test would be the first two books of the *De Anima*, books Z and H of the *Metaphysics*, and book VI of the *Nicomachean Ethics*, works which occupy such a central position in the corpus that if they are not by Aristotle then there is no such person as the Aristotle of philosophical tradition.

Of the nineteen works regarded by scholars as spurious, eight (42.1%) only would be shown to be spurious by this test if used as a test of authorship. This disagreement with the results of scholarship, though greater than that in the case of the genuine works, is less damaging to the value of the test. The users of stylometric tests have always insisted that it is the differences revealed by the tests that are more important than the similarities: if A and B are of a different height, then certainly A is not the same man as B, whereas if A and B are of the same height, it does not follow that A is the same man as B.

Taking the genuine and spurious cases together, we can say that the test agrees with the consensus in seventy-nine cases (64.2%), disagrees in twenty cases (16.3%); whereas either test or consensus is indecisive in twenty-four cases (19.5%).

Though the test cannot be used without further ado as a decision procedure for authorship it would be absurd to reject it for that reason as worthless. Application of the test does after all reveal a habit which is (*a*) locally very consistent in the Aristotelian writings, (*b*) uniform in four-fifths of the works of Aristotle commonly regarded as genuine. The possibility remains open for it to be used as evidence towards the solution of problems concerning immediate local contexts (e.g. whether the disputed books of the *Ethics* belong with the *Eudemian* or *Nicomachean Ethics*; how many strata are to be found in the *Metaphysics*); and for it to be used in conjunction with other tests as an indicator of authorship if it should turn out to correlate well with other tests and if some explanation of the anomalies (e.g. variation over periods of time) should prove to be available. In order to start the exploration of this second possibility, I propose to examine the other suggested test of authorship, applying it once again over the entire Aristotelian corpus.

Before leaving the δέ–γάρ test, however, something should be said about the way in which the test block was built up. After the books had been counted individually, each book was tested against each other book in a large array to see which books were homogeneous with each other and which differed substantially. Inspection of these results suggested both which works were likely, as a whole, to be homogeneous, and which whole works would most closely resemble which other whole works. The homogeneity of the whole works were then tested with the results shown in Table 10.2. The following works were then tested as wholes against each other (i.e. all the samples from a given work were added together to make a large sample representative of that work): *De Caelo, Analytics, Gen* et *Corr,* plus *De Motu* and *De Incessu, Meteorologica, De Partibus Animalium.* This group, each unit of which had been tested and found to be internally homogeneous when tested at the 1% level, yielded as a whole a chi-squared of 7.60 for 8 degrees, thus showing a high degree of homogeneity. The units of the group were then blocked together to make a single big sample containing 778 δέ-sentences, 649 γάρ-sentences, and 574 neither-sentences. This block was then tested with the *Categories*, the *De Interpretatione*, the *Parva Naturalia*, and the *De Generatione Animalium*; the result was a chi-squared of 13.81 for 10 degrees of freedom. The homogeneity shown by this result enabled the group so far constructed to be regarded as a single block containing 1,270 δέ, 1,034 γάρ, 891 neither. To this block was then added, in a similar manner, the samples of *Topics* I–II, V *Physics* with the exception of VII, *Metaphysics* αΒΓΔΙΚ, *NEthics* I–IV VIII–X. This gave a homogeneous block (chi-squared for 48 degrees 60.23) of 2123 δέ, 1,836 γάρ, 1,619 neither, built up of sixty samples from sixty works.

It might be thought that so large a sample could be used without further ado as a test block to be tested against its individual members and against the remainder of the corpus; but it was pointed out to me that the method by which the block had been built up varied the conditions for entry to the block at various stages, and that it might be possible to build up another large homogeneous block of different composition which would give different results. This suggestion was tested, and shown to be correct, by building up a block starting from the *Metaphysics* (which as can be seen from Table 10.2 forms a homogeneous block in itself, with a chi-squared of 38.52 for 26 when samples from the fourteen books are tested against each other). The *Rhetoric* can be added to the *Metaphysics* giving a homogeneous block of 529/514/640 (chi-squared 1.35 for 2); this block plus *Phys* VII and VIII and the disputed books of the *Ethics* gives a further homogeneous block (689/676/818, chi-squared 8.09 for 10), and finally this block plus *Phys* I–V gives a block of 848/852/983, similarly homogeneous (6.37 for 10 degrees). This block if used as a test, gives different results in a number of cases from the first block. The test block finally used in the production of the results shown in Table I was built up by adding together all those samples which tested out as a good fit to *both* the blocks initially chosen, the *Analytics*-based block and the *Metaphysics*-based block. The composition of this final optimum block has already been described. It seems reasonable to regard it as fairly representative of the homogeneous portion of the corpus: but there must be a more mechanical and less subjective method of building up a test block than the hit and miss methods which were actually used.

II

The test based on the syntactic categories of the final words of sentences was chosen for comparison with the δέ–γάρ test because it was a totally independent test, of a different type from those based on the counting of the occurrences of frequent words, which could be conducted and reported in a manner formally quite parallel to the δέ–γάρ test.

Once again each of the 123 books of the corpus was sampled. (The Problems were also studied, but the results of this study are not given here because of the lack of comparable results from the δέ–γάρ test.) The samples consisted commonly of the first one hundred sentences; in forty-one cases, however, the entire work was used as a sample.

The sentences were classified into three groups: those ending in a noun, those ending in a verb, and those ending in some other part of speech. The classification and counting was done by hand; it was not at all easy to attain uniformity in classification. In general words were classified according to form rather than function; a number of general rules were laid down (e.g. that participles were to count as verbs, rather than adjectives); but the classification even so called for quite a number of *ad hoc* decisions. This fact, added to normal human error, meant that it was not uncommon for two different people, or the same person counting the same text on two different occasions, to come up with slightly different results. The Bekker text was again used for the great majority of the samples but (for reasons connected with a different test) the samples from the ethical works were taken from the Bywater edition of the EN (Oxford classical texts) and from the Loeb editions of the *EE* and the *MM*. The possibility of editorial differences therefore must be taken into account in assessing the reliability of the results. Sentences were defined as in the previous test. As this test is fundamentally a method of testing the syntactic features of an author's total use of his vocabulary, last words of sentences being chosen simply as a method of sampling which is particularly sensitive (because of the unlikelihood of the last word being e.g. an article or a particle), the differences between editors concerning punctuation are less important in this test (where sentence length merely determines the point of sampling) than in a test in which sentence length was itself the parameter to be studied.

The results of the counting were tested for statistical significance in the same manner as in the δέ–γάρ test. Internal consistency was normally tested by testing sentences 1–50 against sentences 51–100 of a sample even in cases where the sample consisted of a book as a whole. (Exceptions were the *Categories*, where thirteen fifty-sentence samples were tested against each other, the *Topics*, where three samples were tested against each other in each book, the *Sophistici Elenchi* where nineteen samples were used, the *De Part An* IV were sixteen were used, and the *De Gen An* III where eleven were used). The books composing a single work were tested together for coherence as in the δέ–γάρ test. Among other works, the *Analytics*, the *Physics*, the *De Caelo*, the *De Gen et Corr*, the *De Motu Animalium*, the *De Incessu Animalium*, the *Eudemian Ethics* and the disputed books of the *Ethics* were found to be internally homogeneous in the sense that there was no difference significant at the 1% level between any of the samples taken from these works. The eight samples made by totalling in the case of each work the samples taken from separate books themselves made a homogeneous block of 1,227 sentences ending with nouns, 1,368 ending with verbs, 1,907 ending with other parts of speech (chi-squared 20.5 for 14 degrees of freedom). Adding the samples from the *Rhetoric*, *Metaphysics* AαΓΔZHΘKMN, and *EM* I–III, IX–X with *De Part An* I–III to this block made a further homogeneous block of 1,856/2,073/2,758. This block was then used as a test block to be compared with each of the 123 books in the corpus in turn.

The results of the counting and of the testing for statistical significance are presented in Tables 10.4 and 10.5, in the same manner as for the δέ–γάρ test in Tables 10.1 and 10.2. As in the previous test, the final column of Table 10.4 shows the chi-squared for two degrees of freedom that is obtained by putting the sample in question in a 3 × 2 contingency table with the large sample and testing for statistical significance.

Once again it will be noticed that there is a high degree of local consistency revealed by the testing. Only in seven of the 123 books sampled is there a difference between samples from the same book which is statistically significant at the 1% level. (Cases are italicised in the table.) Four of these anomalous cases are from the *Organon*: namely, *Categories*, *De Interpretatione*, *Topics* I and the *Sophistici Elenchi*. (Two other works from the *Organon*, *Topics* II

Table 10.4.

	Work	Sample	Noun	Verb	Other	Int. Chi[8]	Fit to Block
1	*Categories*	whole	132	310	208	*54.87 for 24*	75.97
2	*De Interp*	whole	80	133	172	*10.36 for 2*	8.97
3	*Anal Pr* I	1–100	31	39	30	0.94 for 2	5.43
4	*Anal Pr* II	do.	29	28	43	3.98 for 2	0.42
5	*Anal Post* I	do.	16	40	44	1.19 for 2	7.68
6	*Anal Post* II	do.	24	40	36	1.79 for 2	3.72
7	*Topics* I	whole	88	151	102	*13.30 for 4*	20.77
8	*Topics* II	do.	70	150	96	*12.02 for 4*	39.96
9	*Topics* III	do.	56	64	103	6.72 for 4	2.54
10	*Topics* IV	do.	112	163	112	*12.11 for 4*	28.14
11	*Topics* V	do.	41	139	248	1.70 for 4	76.68
12	*Topics* VI	do.	122	273	135	9.47 for 4	98.04
13	*Topics* VII	do.	36	67	49	8.44 for 4	11.93
14	*Topics* VIII	do.	95	174	101	6.93 for 4	45.66
15	*Soph El*	whole	253	375	353	*68.52 for 36*	21.03
16	*Physics* I	1–100	18	36	46	3.00 for 2	4.73
17	*Physics* II	do.	33	32	35	0.42 for 2	1.94
18	*Physics* III	do.	25	33	42	1.18 for 2	0.41
19	*Physics* IV	101–200	38	33	39	4.20 for 2	2.71
20	*Physics* V	1–100	31	34	35	0.56 for 2	1.59
21	*Physics* VI	do.	22	26	52	3.82 for 2	4.73
22	*Physics* VII	do.	21	40	39	*18.16 for 2*	4.30
23	*Physics* VIII	do.	21	31	48	1.36 for 2	0.20
24	*De Cael* I	do.	32	21	47	2.96 for 2	4.62
25	*De Cael* II	do.	30	22	48	0.78 for 2	3.85
26	*De Cael* III	do.	32	32	35	1.64 for 2	1.61
27	*De Cael* IV	do.	20	23	57	4.10 for 2	10.08
28	*De G & C* I	do.	30	30	40	3.35 for 2	0.25
29	*De G & C* II	do.	35	22	43	0.04 for 2	4.52
30	*Meteor* I	do.	39	23	38	0.38 for 2	6.76
31	*Meteor* II	do.	35	32	33	5.28 for 2	3.52
32	*Meteor* III	do.	37	30	33	0.20 for 2	4.68
33	*Meteor* IV	do.	31	35	34	0.06 for 2	2.14
34	*De Mundo*	do.	42	36	22	N.A.	7.76
35	*De An* I	whole	129	135	139	1.90 for 2	7.45
36	*De An* II	whole	201	165	135	1.80 for 2	21.18
37	*De An* III	1–100	28	27	45	1.18 for 2	0.85
38	*De S & S*	1–100	39	30	31	1.44 for 2	7.01
39	*De M & R*	whole	49	73	44	0.14 for 2	17.49
40	*De S & V*	1–100	30	40	30	1.07 for 2	5.77
41	*De Som*	1–100	26	40	34	0.60 for 2	3.93
42	*De D per S*	whole	12	35	20	N.A.	14.01
43	*De L & B*	whole	27	29	44	*9.02 for 2*	0.33
44	*De V & H*	whole	37	19	41	N.A.	7.76
45	*De Resp*	1–100	29	40	31	1.54 for 2	5.13
46	*De Spir*	1–100	37	24	39	*6.00 for 2*	4.70
47	*Hst An* I	1–100	53	17	30	0.08 for 2	31.63
48	*Hst An* II	do.	34	17	49	0.66 for 2	9.08
49	*Hst An* III	do.	44	19	37	0.94 for 2	14.32

Table 10.4. (*contd*)

	Work	Sample	Noun	Verb	Other	Int. Chi[8]	Fit to Block
50	*Hst An* IV	do.	47	18	35	0.48 for 2	19.35
51	*Hst An* V	do.	46	17	37	0.08 for 2	18.41
52	*Hst An* VI	do.	39	30	31	4.64 for 2	7.01
53	*Hst An* VII	do.	34	23	43	0.54 for 2	3.50
54	*Hst An* VIII	do.	45	26	27	4.58 for 2	15.62
55	*Hst An* IX	do.	44	17	39	1.86 for 2	15.68
56	*Hst An* X	do.	34	34	32	0.94 for 2	3.71
57	*De P An* I	do.	27	30	43	0.20 for 2	0.13
58	*De P An* II	do.	34	23	43	3.16 for 2	3.50
59	*De P An* III	do.	37	35	28	0.05 for 2	7.74
60	*De P An* IV	whole	371	175	260	35.16 for 30	115.13
61	*De Mot An*	1.100	25	34	41	3.86 for 2	0.77
62	*De Inc An*	1–100	28	28	46	3.20 for 2	0.56
63	*De Gen An* I	do.	46	24	30	1.20 for 2	16.30
64	*De Gen An* II	do.	28	35	37	1.10 for 2	0.58
65	*De Gen An* III	whole	221	124	210	34.44 for 20	40.12
66	*De Gen An* IV	1–100	30	35	35	3.36 for 2	1.62
67	*De Gen An* V	1–100	28	39	33	4.53 for 2	3.66
68	*De Color*	1–100	39	39	22	1.28 for 2	15.40
69	*De Audib*	do.	46	24	30	0.25 for 2	14.12
70	*Physiogn*	do.	26	48	26	2.13 for 2	14.80
71	*De Plant* I	do.	39	32	29	*11.77 for 2*	8.09
72	*De Plant* II	do.	37	28	35	0.84 for 2	4.24
73	*De Mir Aus*	do.	32	47	21	1.40 for 2	18.57
74	*Mechan*	do.	30	15	55	0.22 for 2	12.88
75	*De Lin Ins*	do.	29	29	42	4.11 for 2	5.50
76	*Vent Sit*	whole	36	11	3	N.A.	50.95
77	*De Meliss*	1–100	8	53	39	N.A.	29.13
78	*Metaph* A	1–100	35	36	29	0.06 for 2	6.25
79	*Metaph* α	whole	17	30	23	*6.05 for 2*	4.61
80	*Metaph* B	whole	75	91	128	0.73 for 2	1.05
81	*Metaph* Γ	1–100	32	28	40	0.73 for 2	0.96
82	*Metaph* Δ	1–100	38	25	37	0.84 for 2	5.28
83	*Metaph* E	whole	16	48	46	N.A.	12.40
84	*Metaph* Z	1–100	24	33	43	1.02 for 2	0.70
85	*Metaph* H	whole	67	56	64	3.40 for 2	6.49
86	*Metaph* Θ	whole	68	108	124	3.54 for 2	5.00
87	*Metaph* I	whole	72	77	175	3.36 for 2	20.76
88	*Metaph* K	whole	111	136	181	5.98 for 2	0.67
89	*Metaph* Λ	1–100	37	18	46	1.29 for 2	8.07
90	*Metaph* M	1–100	35	24	41	5.00 for 2	3.42
91	*Metaph* N	1–100	24	31	45	5.28 for 2	3.66
92	*E Nic* I	whole	89	129	148	3.06 for 2	3.55
93	*E Nic* II	whole	68	91	82	3.74 for 2	6.38
94	*E Nic* III	whole	113	164	159	2.40 for 2	8.86
95	*E Nic* IV	whole	67	204	174	2.56 for 2	54.21
96	*E Nic* V	whole	85	128	184	1.48 for 2	8.04
97	*E Nic* VI	whole	85	96	103	1.22 for 2	2.79
98	*E Nic* VII	whole	114	112	159	*7.94 for 2*	0.88

99	*E Nic* VIII	whole	107	171	165	2.04 for 2	13.04
100	*E Nic* IX	whole	41	195	127	1.58 for 2	93.21
101	*E Nic* X	whole	120	158	137	3.00 for 2	2.91
102	*M Mor* I	whole	205	319	344	1.00 for 2	13.33
103	*M Mor* II	whole	174	322	257	0.04 for 2	42.90
104	*E Eud* I	whole	41	38	63	*7.30 for 2*	1.20
105	*E Eud* II	whole	125	113	138	0.38 for 2	5.50
106	*E Eud* III	whole	55	75	105	3.08 for 2	2.27
107	*E Eud* VII	whole	171	204	308	0.50 for 2	4.13
108	*De V & V*	whole	40	15	19	N.A.	25.10
109	*Pol* I	whole	107	100	117	1.92 for 2	5.05
110	*Pol* II	whole	196	143	199	0.08 for 2	18.57
111	*Pol* III	whole	187	122	209	6.20 for 2	20.66
112	*Pol* IV	1–100	32	24	44	0.26 for 2	2.38
113	*Pol* V	do.	32	22	46	63.06 for 2	3.43
114	*Pol* VI	do.	37	22	41	1.14 for 2	4.61
115	*Pol* VII	whole	180	146	192	5.36 for 2	11.61
116	*Pol* VIII	1–100	31	28	41	1.09 for 2	0.66
117	*Econ* I	whole	33	36	36	1.10 for 2	2.58
118	*Econ* II	1–100	28	48	24	0.30 for 2	16.26
119	*Rhet* I	do.	28	32	40	5.06 for 2	0.01
120	*Rhet* II	do.	20	45	35	1.28 for 2	9.27
121	*Rhet* III	do.	32	33	35	1.77 for 2	1.70
122	*Rh ad Al*	do.	27	52	21	*8.05 for 2*	23.76
123	*Post*	do.	57	28	55	5.07 for 2	22.79

and IV are inconsistent if tested at the 5% level.) This inconsistency may perhaps be explained by the frequency of sentences and arguments used as examples in these logical works; examples which, as scholars have often suggested, may not be of Aristotle's own composition but be part of Academic tradition. It would be interesting to test this hypothesis by collecting the statistics for these works minus the examples. The fifth anomaly, *Physics* VII, is a book whose textual history is uniquely complicated and whose anomalous nature was also detected by the δέ–γάρ test. Here, as in the δέ–γάρ test, there remain two anomalous cases for which no obvious explanation presents itself: the fifth book of the *Politics* and the first book of the spurious *De Plantis*. In addition to the two books of the *Topics* already mentioned there are seven books (emphasized) which display internal differences significant at the 5% level (*De Long. et Brev, De Gen. An G, Met α, EN H, EE A, Rhet ad Al*. and the spurious *De Spiritu*).

As will be seen from Table 10.5, the individual works of the corpus do not display as high a degree of homogeneity between individual books of a single work as was found in the δέ–γάρ test.

Table 10.5.

Work	No. Samples	Noun	Verb	Other	Chi.[8]	Significance
Categories	13	132	310	208	54.87 for 24	1
De Interp	2	80	133	172	10.36 for 2	1
Prior Anal	2	60	67	73	4.19 for 2	0
Post Anal	2	40	80	80	2.40 for 2	0
Topics	8	620	1,179	945	180.67 for 14	1
Soph El	19	253	375	353	68.52 for 35	1
Physics	8	209	245	336	20.60 for 14	0
De Cael	4	124	98	187	11.87 for 6	0
De G & C	2	65	52	83	1.72 for 2	0
Meteor	4	143	130	138	4.08 for 6	0
De Mundo	2	40	34	26	1.08 for 2	0
De Anima	3	358	327	369	7.26 for 4	0
Parva Naturalia	8	134	287	234	36.19 for 14	1
De Spiritu	2	37	24	39	6.00 for 2	5
Hist An	18	420	220	360	36.64 for 18	1
Part An	4	469	263	374	24.28 for 6	1
De Mot An	2	25	34	41	3.86 for 2	0
De Inc An	2	28	28	46	3.20 for 2	0
De Gen An	5	353	257	345	39.81 for 8	1
De Color	2	39	39	22	1.28 for 2	0
De Audib	2	46	24	30	0.25 for 2	0
Physiogn	2	26	48	26	2.13 for 2	0
De Plant	2	76	60	64	0.88 for 2	0
De Mir Aus	2	32	47	21	1.40 for 2	0
Mechan	2	30	15	55	0.22 for 2	0
De Lin Ins	2	29	29	42	4.11 for 2	0
De Meliss	2	8	53	39	N.A.	
Metaphysics	14	604	648	958	88.82 for 26	1
Nic Ethics	7	599	1,112	992	72.28 for 12	1
Disputed Bks	3	284	336	445	11.82 for 4	5
Magna Moralia	2	379	641	601	7.02 for 2	5
Eudemian Ethics	5	392	430	615	12.57 for 8	0
De V & V	2	40	25	19	N.A.	
Politics	8	702	585	889	11.80 for 14	0
Economica	2	61	84	60	4.40 for 2	0
Rhetoric	3	80	130	110	5.27 for 4	0
Rhet ad Al	2	27	52	21	8.05 for 2	5
Poetics	2	57	28	55	5.07 for 2	0

In that earlier test, only the *Topics* and the *De Hist Animalium* betrayed inconsistency if tested at the 1% level. Both inconsistencies were readily explained: the *Topics* for the reason already given in connection with the internal inconsistency; the *Hist An* because it has long been regarded by scholars, on internal evidence, as an album to which many hands contributed. By the present test, both of these works are similarly inconsistent at the

1% level; but so too are the *Categories*, the *De Interpretatione*, and, outside the *Organon*, the *Parva Naturalia*, the *De Partibus Animalium*, the *De Generatione Animalium*, the *Metaphysics* and the *Nicomachean Ethics*. These inconsistencies can usually be traced to individual books or pairs of books, whose removal leaves a coherent whole (thus in the *Parva Naturalia* the work *De Vita et Morte* seems to stand out; in the *De Partibus* book IV; in the *De Generatione* book III; in the *Metaphysics* books E and I, and in the *Nicomachean Ethics* IV and IX.)

The results of the Last Word test show less agreement with the consensus of scholarship than do the results of the δέ–γάρ test. The Last Word test agrees with the consensus in sixty-three cases (51.2%), disagrees with it in thirty-two cases (26.0%), and either it or the consensus is indecisive in twenty-eight cases.

All the reservations which were expressed above about the possibility of using the earlier test as a test of authorship apply with stronger force in the present case. Not only is the gap between the test and the scholarly consensus larger, but the test block was not tested for representativeness in the same way as in the earlier case. If the Last Word test were used in a crude way as a test of authorship, such unquestioned works as books IV and IX of the *Nicomachean Ethics* and the second and third books of the *Politics* would have to be rejected. None the less, the application of the test reveals a number of interesting facts which do seem to call for explanation: the anomalousness of the *Topics*, revealed by this test no less clearly than by the δέ–γάρ test, the close uniformity of the *Physics, Analytics*, and zoological works, and the sharp divergence of two books of the *Nicomachean Ethics* from the pattern to be observed in their context.

III

If the application of the δέ–γάρ test and of the Last Word test to the Aristotelian corpus is severally inconclusive, can the two tests be taken together to reveal an indicator of authorship?

If an affirmative answer is to be given there must be a considerable degree of agreement between the two tests in the results they yield. We find in fact that of the 123 cases in which the tests were applied, they agreed with each other in seventy cases (56.9%) and disagreed with each other in twenty-eight cases (22.8%). In the remaining twenty-five cases (20.3% of the total) one or other of the tests was indecisive in the sense of giving a result which showed a difference from the sample block at a level between the 1% and the 5% significance levels.

Of the seventy cases in which the tests agreed, their common results agreed with the consensus of scholarship in fifty-one cases (72.8%), disagreed with it in nine cases (12.9%) and in the remaining ten cases (14.3%) there was no consensus among scholars on the status of the work.

The comparison between the results of the individual tests, and between their consensus and the consensus of scholarship, is set out in Table 10.6. That table shows what would be the result if each of the tests, were used—as I have argued they should not be used—as crude tests of authorship, with a result of no statistical significance indicating the genuineness of the work, a result of significance at the 1% level indicating the spuriousness of the work, and a result between the 5% level and the 1% level leaving the status of the work doubtful. In the third column a work is indicated as genuine if shown as genuine by both stylistic tests, spurious if shown as spurious by both stylistic tests, and otherwise as doubtful.

As the table shows, there are in the end nine cases in which the stylistic tests agree with each other against the consensus of scholarship. There are three cases in which works commonly regarded as spurious appear genuine on the tests: namely, the *De Spiritu*, the *De Lineis Insecabilibus*, and the first book of the *Economica*. The arguments advanced by scholars for the inauthenticity of these books do not appear to me at all conclusive; on the other hand, even if the stylistic tests had been validated much more strictly than has proved to be possible, the similarity between these books and the major part of the Aristotelian corpus in respect of these features of style would be rather a weak argument for authenticity.

There are six cases where works regarded by scholars as genuine appear spurious on the tests: four books of the *Topics* (I, IV, VI, VIII), *De Anima* II, *Rhetoric* II. The reasons for regarding these works as authentic appear to me sufficiently strong to show that these results alone invalidate the tests unless (as I have tried to suggest in the case of the *Topics*) particular explanations of the anomalies can be given.

Table 10.6.

	Work	δέ–γάρ Test	NVO Test	Stylistic Test	Scholarly Concensus
1	*Categories*	Genuine	Spurious	Doubtful	Doubtful
2	*De Interp*	Doubtful	Doubtful	Doubtful	Genuine
3	*Anal Pr* I	Genuine	Genuine	Genuine	Genuine
4	*Anal Pr* II	Genuine	Genuine	Genuine	Genuine
5	*An Post* I	Genuine	Doubtful	Doubtful	Genuine
6	*An Post* II	Genuine	Genuine	Genuine	Genuine
7	*Topics* I	Spurious	Spurious	Spurious	Genuine
8	*Topics* II	Genuine	Spurious	Doubtful	Genuine
9	*Topics* III	Doubtful	Genuine	Doubtful	Genuine
10	*Topics* IV	Spurious	Spurious	Spurious	Genuine
11	*Topics* V	Doubtful	Spurious	Doubtful	Doubtful
12	*Topics* VI	Spurious	Spurious	Spurious	Genuine
13	*Topics* VII	Genuine	Spurious	Doubtful	Genuine
14	*Topics* VIII	Spurious	Spurious	Spurious	Genuine
15	*Soph El*	Genuine	Spurious	Doubtful	Genuine
16	*Physics* I	Genuine	Genuine	Genuine	Genuine
17	*Physics* II	Genuine	Genuine	Genuine	Genuine
18	*Physics* III	Genuine	Genuine	Genuine	Genuine
19	*Physics* IV	Genuine	Genuine	Genuine	Genuine
20	*Physics* V	Genuine	Genuine	Genuine	Genuine
21	*Physics* VI	Genuine	Genuine	Genuine	Genuine
22	*Physics* VII	Doubtful	Genuine	Doubtful	Genuine
23	*Physics* VIII	Genuine	Genuine	Genuine	Genuine
24	*De Cael* I	Genuine	Genuine	Genuine	Genuine
25	*De Cael* II	Genuine	Genuine	Genuine	Genuine
26	*De Cael* III	Genuine	Genuine	Genuine	Genuine
27	*De Cael* IV	Genuine	Spurious	Doubtful	Genuine
28	*De G & C* I	Genuine	Genuine	Genuine	Genuine
29	*De G & C* II	Genuine	Genuine	Genuine	Genuine
30	*Meteor* I	Genuine	Doubtful	Doubtful	Genuine
31	*Meteor* II	Genuine	Genuine	Genuine	Genuine
32	*Meteor* III	Genuine	Genuine	Genuine	Genuine
33	*Meteor* IV	Genuine	Genuine	Genuine	Doubtful
34	*De Mundo*	Spurious	Spurious	Spurious	Spurious
35	*De An* I	Spurious	Doubtful	Doubtful	Genuine
36	*De An* II	Spurious	Spurious	Spurious	Genuine
37	*De An* III	Genuine	Genuine	Genuine	Genuine
38	*De S & S*	Genuine	Doubtful	Genuine	Genuine
39	*De M & R*	Genuine	Spurious	Doubtful	Genuine
40	*De S & V*	Genuine	Genuine	Genuine	Genuine
41	*De Som*	Genuine	Genuine	Genuine	Genuine
42	*De D p S*	Genuine	Spurious	Doubtful	Genuine
43	*De L & S*	Genuine	Genuine	Genuine	Genuine
44	*De V & M*	Genuine	Doubtful	Doubtful	Genuine
45	*De Resp*	Genuine	Genuine	Genuine	Genuine
46	*De Spir*	Genuine	Genuine	Genuine	Spurious
47	*Hst An* I	Spurious	Spurious	Spurious	Doubtful
48	*Hst An* II	Spurious	Doubtful	Doubtful	Doubtful
49	*Hst An* III	Spurious	Spurious	Spurious	Doubtful

Table 10.6. (*contd*)

	Work	δέ–γάρ Test	NVO Test	Stylistic Test	Scholarly Concensus
50	*Hst An* IV	Spurious	Spurious	Spurious	Doubtful
51	*Hst An* V	Spurious	Spurious	Spurious	Doubtful
52	*Hst An* VI	Spurious	Doubtful	Doubtful	Doubtful
53	*Hst An* VII	Doubtful	Genuine	Doubtful	Spurious
54	*Hst An* VIII	Spurious	Spurious	Spurious	Doubtful
55	*Hst An* IX	Doubtful	Spurious	Doubtful	Spurious
56	*Hst An* X	Spurious	Genuine	Doubtful	Spurious
57	*De P An* I	Genuine	Genuine	Genuine	Genuine
58	*De P An* II	Genuine	Genuine	Genuine	Genuine
59	*De P An* III	Spurious	Doubtful	Doubtful	Genuine
60	*De P An* IV	Genuine	Spurious	Doubtful	Genuine
61	*De M An*	Genuine	Genuine	Genuine	Genuine
62	*De I An*	Genuine	Genuine	Genuine	Genuine
63	*De Gen An* I	Genuine	Spurious	Doubtful	Genuine
64	*De Gen An* II	Genuine	Genuine	Genuine	Genuine
65	*De Gen An* III	Genuine	Spurious	Doubtful	Genuine
66	*De Gen An* IV	Genuine	Genuine	Genuine	Genuine
67	*De Gen An* V	Genuine	Genuine	Genuine	Genuine
68	*De Color*	Genuine	Spurious	Doubtful	Spurious
69	*De Audib*	Spurious	Spurious	Spurious	Spurious
70	*Physiogn*	Doubtful	Spurious	Doubtful	Spurious
71	*De Plant* I	Spurious	Doubtful	Doubtful	Spurious
72	*De Plant* II	Doubtful	Genuine	Doubtful	Spurious
73	*De Mir Aug*	Spurious	Spurious	Spurious	Spurious
74	*Mechan*	Genuine	Spurious	Doubtful	Spurious
75	*De Lin Inc*	Genuine	Genuine	Genuine	Spurious
76	*Vent Sit*	Spurious	Spurious	Spurious	Spurious
77	*De Meliss*	Genuine	Spurious	Doubtful	Spurious
78	*Metaph* A	Genuine	Doubtful	Doubtful	Genuine
79	*Metaph* α	Genuine	Genuine	Genuine	Doubtful
80	*Metaph* B	Genuine	Genuine	Genuine	Genuine
81	*Metaph* Γ	Genuine	Genuine	Genuine	Genuine
82	*Metaph* Δ	Genuine	Genuine	Genuine	Genuine
83	*Metaph* E	Spurious	Spurious	Spurious	Doubtful
84	*Metaph* Z	Spurious	Genuine	Doubtful	Genuine
85	*Metaph* H	Spurious	Doubtful	Doubtful	Genuine
86	*Metaph* Θ	Genuine	Genuine	Genuine	Genuine
87	*Metaph* I	Genuine	Spurious	Doubtful	Genuine
88	*Metaph* K	Genuine	Genuine	Genuine	Doubtful
89	*Metaph* Λ	Spurious	Doubtful	Doubtful	Genuine
90	*Metaph* M	Doubtful	Genuine	Doubtful	Genuine
91	*Metaph* N	Spurious	Genuine	Doubtful	Genuine
92	*E Nic* I	Genuine	Genuine	Genuine	Genuine
93	*E Nic* II	Genuine	Doubtful	Doubtful	Genuine
94	*E Nic* III	Genuine	Doubtful	Doubtful	Genuine
95	*E Nic* IV	Genuine	Spurious	Doubtful	Genuine
96	*E Nic* V	Genuine	Doubtful	Doubtful	Genuine
97	*E Nic* VI	Spurious	Genuine	Doubtful	Genuine
98	*E Nic* VII	Doubtful	Genuine	Doubtful	Genuine

99	*E Nic* VIII	Genuine	Spurious	Doubtful	Genuine
100	*E Nic* IX	Genuine	Spurious	Doubtful	Genuine
101	*E Nic* X	Genuine	Spurious	Doubtful	Genuine
102	*MMA*	Spurious	Spurious	Spurious	Doubtful
103	*MMB*	Genuine	Spurious	Doubtful	Doubtful
104	*E Eud* I	Genuine	Genuine	Genuine	Genuine
105	*E Eud* II	Genuine	Genuine	Genuine	Genuine
106	*E Eud* III	Genuine	Genuine	Genuine	Genuine
107	*E Eud* VII	Genuine	Genuine	Genuine	Genuine
108	*De V & V*	Spurious	Spurious	Spurious	Spurious
109	*Pol* I	Genuine	Genuine	Genuine	Genuine
110	*Pol* II	Genuine	Spurious	Doubtful	Genuine
111	*Pol* III	Genuine	Spurious	Doubtful	Genuine
112	*Pol* IV	Genuine	Spurious	Doubtful	Genuine
113	*Pol* V	Genuine	Genuine	Genuine	Genuine
114	*Pol* VI	Genuine	Genuine	Genuine	Genuine
115	*Pol* VII	Genuine	Spurious	Doubtful	Genuine
116	*Pol* VIII	Genuine	Genuine	Genuine	Genuine
117	*Econ* I	Genuine	Genuine	Genuine	Spurious
118	*Econ* II	Spurious	Spurious	Spurious	Spurious
119	*Rhet* I	Genuine	Genuine	Genuine	Genuine
120	*Rhet* II	Spurious	Spurious	Spurious	Genuine
121	*Rhet* III	Genuine	Genuine	Genuine	Genuine
122	*Rh ad Al*	Genuine	Spurious	Doubtful	Spurious
123	*Poet*	Genuine	Spurious	Doubtful	Genuine

In cases where the consensus of scholars is doubtful, the tests give the following results: *Meteorologica* IV, *Metaphysics* α and *Metaphysics* K are genuine; *Hist An* I, III, IV, V, VIII, *Metaph* E, *Magna Moralia* I are spurious. Each of these results appears to me, as an Aristotelian scholar, to be entirely credible. But as a novice stylometrist I cannot yet claim any high degree of confidence in the manner in which they have been attained.

11

A Stylometric Comparison between Five Disputed Works and the Remainder of the Aristotelian Corpus

What can stylometric techniques tell us about the authenticity of the five possibly Aristotelian works which are our topic?[1] In the present state of our knowledge it is not easy to give a precise answer to this question. There is no doubt, to my mind, that the statistical examination of literary style is a valuable auxiliary tool in the study of the questions which interest the philogist and the philosopher who approach an ancient text. But to decide whether a work is genuine or spurious is one of the most difficult tasks for stylometry.

In my book *The Aristotelian Ethics* (Oxford, 1978) I made use of stylometric methods in an attempt to decide whether the disputed books of the Aristotelian ethics belong to the *Nicomachean* or the *Eudemian Ethics*. This was a problem of a very simple structure. Whether a text A resembles a text B more than it resembles a text C in certain respects is something which can be objectively ascertained and precisely measured. Moreover, the choice of the respects to be measured was dictated by the nature of the problem itself: it was a matter of empirical investigation to discover which features of vocabulary discriminated between the *Nicomachean* and the *Eudemian Ethics* and which, therefore, were the features which should be investigated in the disputed books for purposes of comparison. The investigation of the problem involved no assumptions about the degree of variability of style to be found in an author over periods of time and differences of genre. For these and other reasons I regard the conclusion of that stylometric

---

[1] The *Categories*, the fourth book of the *Meteorologica*, the *De Motu Animalium*, and books α and K of the Metaphysics.

inquiry—that the disputed books fit the Eudemian context much better than the Nicomachean one—as solidly established.

Matters are very different when we attempt to use stylometric methods to settle questions of authenticity. We may find, easily enough, that in respect of certain measurable features a dubious work differs to a marked degree from the major part of the Aristotelian corpus; but we have no *a priori* method of deciding *how far* a text can differ from the rest of the corpus and yet be genuine Aristotle. Again, if we wish to discover whether *Metaph.* α is by Aristotle or by Pasicles of Rhodes we do not have any way of knowing in advance which are the features of language we should be examining; not having any of the works of Pasicles we cannot look for discriminators between his style and Aristotle's, as we can comb the two *Ethics* for their favourite words and idioms to act as tell-tales. The only way in which we can find how far Aristotle varies his usages from work to work is by a study of the entire authentic corpus; and the only way in which we can find out which features are particularly characteristic of him is by comparing those features which are found to be reasonably constant throughout the authentic corpus with the works of other comparable Greek authors. We cannot arbitrarily define Aristotle as the author of some single work—say *Int.* or *Part. An.*—and then regard every statistically significant difference of usage in another work in the corpus as evidence of spuriousness. We cannot do this unless we know what degree of variability is to be found within genuine Aristotle—that is to say, within the greater part of the corpus; for if there is no single person who is the author of the greater part of the corpus, then there is no such person as the Aristotle of tradition. Nor, on the other hand, can we decide that a work which resembles the greater part of the corpus in all the features we have selected for study is therefore a genuine work of Aristotle: unless we study the work also of other authors we have no idea whether the selected features are features common to the Greek of a particular time and genre, or whether they are uniquely characteristic of Aristotle himself.

A firm stylometric conclusion about the authenticity of the works considered here would have to be based on a truly gigantic amount of investigation: investigation which would take a very long time even now when machine-readable texts of Aristotle are available and when computers will produce concordances, word counts, and statistical analyses with a modicum of effort. The present essay offers only a minute contribution to such an investigation. It studies the use of twenty-four common particles and connectives in the dubious works, comparing the four commonest of them with virtually the whole Aristotelian corpus, and the other twenty with a large sample of some 300,000 words, which constitute about 30 per cent of the round million words of the entire corpus. The essay will provide only tentative indications of the genuineness or spuriousness of the works in dispute; but it will illustrate the difficulties and pitfalls of the use of stylometric methods in authorship attribution studies.

I

The four commonest particles in the Aristotelian corpus are καί, δέ, γάρ, and μέν, in that order. Between them these four particles constitute around 14 per cent of a typical Aristotelian text. Because of their frequency and topic-neutrality they provide suitable material for statistical study. We shall use them as a starting-point for a comparison between the dubious works and the rest of the Aristotelian corpus.

Table 11.1 sets out the rates of occurrence of these particles in the five works in question.[2] For each work the table gives first the absolute number of occurrences of the particle, and then the relative frequency: that is to say, the proportion of the total word-tokens in the text which are occurrences of the particle in question. (In order to avoid a superfluity of noughts the proportions are given as percentages: thus the proportion of καί in the *Categories* is 0.0519, and this is shown in the table as 5.19%.) Attached to each proportion is the standard error of that proportion. The standard error of a proportion is a measure of the reliability of the proportion in a sample as an indicator of the proportion in a larger population from which the sample is

---

[2] The word-counts on which the tables in this article are based were made on the Oxford University LCL 1906A computer by the COCOA concordance and word-count program written at the ATLAS computing laboratory; they are derived from machine-readable texts of Aristotle's works prepared by the Thesaurus Linguae Graecae of Irvine, Calif. The correlation matrices in Figures 11.1 and 11.2 were made by the FAKAD statistical package at Oxford.

Table 11.1. *The four commonest particles in five dubious works of Aristotle*

Particle	Cat.			Mete. IV			Mot. An.			Metaph. α			Metaph. K		
	No.	%	SE	No.	%	SE	No.	%	SE	No.	%	SE.	No.	%	SE
καί	530	5.19	0.21	523	6.90	0.29	244	5.92	0.37	41	3.53	0.54	346	4.85	0.25
δέ	386	3.77	0.19	412	5.43	0.26	176	4.27	0.31	45	3.87	0.57	317	4.44	0.24
γάρ	263	2.57	0.16	144	1.89	0.16	73	1.77	0.21	35	3.01	0.50	159	2.23	0.17
μέν	141	1.38	0.12	177	2.33	0.17	75	1.82	0.21	17	1.46	0.35	92	1.29	0.13
Total words in book	10,213			7,583			4,120			1,162			7,132		

For each book is given first the absolute number of occurrences of the particle, followed by the proportion in per cent, followed by the appropriate standard error.

drawn. A larger sample is a more reliable indicator of the underlying population than a smaller: this is reflected in the fact that (as will be seen in the table) the proportions in a small book like *Metaph.* α are accompanied by a larger standard error than the proportions in a large book like *Cat.* The standard error is in fact calculated according to the formula $\sqrt{p(1-p)/n}$, where p is the proportion, and n the number of words in the text.

The way in which the standard error acts as the indicator of the reliability of a sample is this. If two samples are drawn randomly from a homogeneous population, it can be calculated mathematically that the proportion in one sample will not differ from the proportion in the other by more than twice the sum of their standard errors more than once in twenty times. Consequently, if two sample proportions differ by more than this amount, the odds are about twenty to one that they do not come from a single homogeneous population. If everything that Aristotle wrote formed a homogeneous whole in respect of particle usage we would expect the vast majority of his writings to exhibit particle frequencies which did not differ from each other by more than twice the sum of their standard errors.

Of course, the assumption that all Aristotle's writing is homogeneous in respect of particle usage is an unrealistic one: just how unrealistic we shall see in the course of this paper. But the use of statistical methods in the study of his style does not presuppose that his usage is homogeneous. On the contrary, the statistical theorems which lie behind the use of the standard error in drawing inferences from sample to underlying population provide us with a method of measuring the lack of homogeneity. For by telling us what Aristotle's writings would look like if each book of each of his works could be regarded as a random sample from a homogeneous whole, they tell us how much of the variation which they actually display can be attributed to chance fluctuation and how much of it is due to genuine stylistic differences.

To illustrate this let us look at the differences in the frequency of καί in table 11.1. The rate in the *Cat.*, 5.19, differs from that in *Metaph.* K, 4.85. However, the difference between the two rates, 0.34, is well within twice the sum of the respective standard errors: $(0.21 + 0.25) \times 2 = 0.92$. Hence, there is no need to look for any explanation for the difference between the frequencies: it is the same kind of difference as the difference between two honestly dealt bridge hands from a fair pack of cards. On the other hand, the difference between the *Mot. An.* and *Metaph.* α (2.39) is much more than twice the sum of the standard errors (1.82); hence it cannot be regarded as a random fluctuation but must be treated as statistically significant. *Mot. An.* and *Metaph.* α cannot be regarded as two samples from a single population homogeneous in respect of καί usage. That does not mean, of course, that they cannot be regarded as two works of the same author; all it means is that an explanation of the difference is called for. But many kinds of explanation would suffice: a difference in date, or genre, or a conscious decision of an author to vary his style, for instance. In order to judge the plausibility of this kind of explanation we need further information about the degree of variation which authors display in speech habits of this kind; and this is something which calls for empirical inquiry, and not merely the use of the *a priori* calculus of probability.

We are primarily interested not in comparing these dubious works with each other, but in comparing them with the overall Aristotelian corpus. Figures are available for particle frequency in a large sample of the corpus, consisting of the *Metaph.*, *EN*, *EE*, *Pol.*, *An.* and *Rhet.* in their entireties, a sample of 291,588 words. Let us now compare the frequencies for each of the dubious books with these Aristotelian proportions. *Cat.* differs from the Aristotelian sample by more than twice the sum of the standard errors in every case except that of μέν, *Mete.* in every case except γάρ. *Mot. An.* is in every case easily within these limits. Of *Metaph.*

Table 11.2. *The frequencies of the four particles in the sample*

	Frequency	Standard error
καί	6.00	0.04
δέ	4.00	0.04
γάϱ	2.16	0.03
μέν	1.62	0.02

book α is outside the limits in the case of καί and K in the case of καί and μέν.

The one fact which emerges clearly from this comparison is that no case could be made against the authenticity of the *Mot. An.* on the basis of its usage of these particles; indeed its closeness to the Aristotelian paradigm is striking in contrast to the performance of the other works.

But we have a long way to go yet before we can decide whether the statistically significant differences between the usages in the other books offer any evidence of diversity of authorship. We have to ascertain what degree of diversity in the usage of these particles is to be found between undoubtedly authentic works of Aristotle. This we shall now do for each of these particles in turn.

Table 11.3 shows the frequency of καί in one hundred Aristotelian or pseudo-Aristotelian texts. The works for which values are given are: each individual book of the *Organon,* of *Phys.,* of *Cael.,* of *Gener. Corr.,* of *Mete.,* of *An.; Part. An., Mot. An.* and *Inc. An.* as wholes, the books of *Gener. An.* with books IV and V taken together; each individual book of *Metaph.,* of *EN* and *EE; MM* as a whole; each individual book of *Pol.* and *Rhet.; Somn., Insomn., Div. Somn., Long., Juv., Respir., Spir., Col., Aud., Mech., Lin., Vent., Epist., Ath. Pol.,* and *Protrepticus.*

The table shows at once the very great amount of variation in Aristotle's usage of καί. Unquestioned works by Aristotle differ by a greater amount than the difference between *Mete.* IV and *Metaph.* α in Table 11.1. Thus three books of *EN* and two of *Rhet.* have a καί-frequency greater than that of the former, and the first book of *Anal. Pr.* has a frequency less than that of the latter. It would thus be rash to draw conclusions about the authenticity of these works on the basis of καί-usage alone.

Table 11.3. *Proportion of* καί *in works of Aristotle*

8.0+	*Virt., Col.*
7.8	
7.6	
7.4	*EN* I, *Rhet.* I
7.2	*EN* IV, *Spir., Aud.*
7.0	*EN* II, *Rhet.* II
6.8	*Mete.* IV
6.6	*EE* II, III
6.4	*Gener. Corr.* II, *Pol.* I, *Somn., Insomn.*
6.2	*Phys.* II, *Metaph.* H, *EN* III, VIII, X, *EE* VIII, *Long.*
6.0	*An.* III, *Metaph.* Δ, Θ, *EN* VII, IX, *EE* VII, *Pol.* VIII
5.8	*Phys.* I, *Cael.* IV, *Gener. Corr.* I, *Mot. An., Metaph.* A, Γ, Z, I, M, *EN* VI, *Protrept.*
5.6	*Phys.* III, IV, V, *Mete.* II, *An.* II, *Part. An., Gener. An.* II, IV–V, *Metaph.* Λ, N, *EN* V, *Pol.* VI, VII, *Ath. Pol.*
5.4	*Top.* VII, *Phys.* VII, *Mete.* I, *An.* I, *Gener. An.* III, *Metaph.* B, *Pol.* V
5.2	*Top.* III, *Gener. An.* I, *Pol.* IV, *Rhet.* III, *Div. Somn., Epist.*
5.0	*Cat., Top.* II, IV, *Phys.* VIII, *Cael.* I, *Inc. An., MM*
4.8	*Metaph.* K, *EE* I, *Pol.* II, III, *Lin.*
4.6	*Top.* I, *Cael.* III, *Mete.* III, *Juv., Respir., Vent.*
4.4	*Int., Soph. El., Phys.* VI, *Cael.* II, *Metaph.* E
4.2	
4.0	
3.8	*Anal. Pr.* II, *Anal. Post.* I, II
3.6	
3.4	*Top.* VIII, *Metaph.* α
3.2	*Top.* VI
3.0	*Anal. Pr.* I, *Mech.*
2.8	
2.6	
2.4	*Top.* V

Values between n.m0 and n.(m + 1)9 appear on the line headed n.m.

None the less, a certain pattern does emerge from the distribution as a whole. Logical works score low, ethical and rhetorical works score high; physical and zoological works tend to be, with *Metaph.*, near the average. *Mete.* IV scores higher than any genuine book of comparable subject-matter, and *Metaph.* α scores well below any other book of that work. It is noticeable that the texts which occur at the extreme ends of the distribution are all questionable: the highest scorers are the spurious *Virt.* and *Col.*; the two lowest scorers are the spurious *Mech.* and *Top.* V which has been questioned by scholars on quite other grounds.

Table 11.4 shows the frequency of δέ in the same one hundred works. Here it will be seen that the figure recorded for *Mete.* IV, 5.43, is one of the two highest in the corpus; it is exceeded only by the maverick *Vent.* (8.69); at the other end of the scale we again find two questionable works, the spurious *Epistles*, and the

Table 11.4. *Proportion of* δέ *in works of Aristotle*

5.4+	*Mete.* IV, *Vent.*
5.3	
5.2	
5.1	*An.* II, *EN* VIII
5.0	*An.* I, *EN* II
4.9	*Anal. Pr.* II, *EN* IV
4.8	*Pol.* IV
4.7	*Gener. An.* IV–V, *EN* I, *Ath. Pol.*
4.6	*Cael.* IV, *Part. An.*
4.5	
4.4	*Mete.* III, *Metaph.* K, *EN* VII, IX
4.3	*Anal. Post.* I, *Inc. An.*, *Gener. An.* III, *Metaph.* H, *EN* V, *Somn.*, *Juv.*
4.2	*Anal. Pr.* I, *Phys.* V, *Gener. Corr.* I, II, *Mot. An.*, *EE* III, VII, *Rhet.* III, *Long.*
4.1	*Top.* I, *Gener. An.* II, *Pol.* VI
4.0	*Top.* VIII, *Phys.* VIII, *Cael.* III, *Metaph.* Δ, Θ, *EE* II, *Rhet.* I, *Respir.*, *Spir.*, *Lin.*
3.9	*Anal. Post.* II, *Metaph.* Λ, *Pol.* I
3.8	*Phys.* IV, *Mete.* II, *Metaph.* α, E, *EN* VI, X, *Pol.* II, V
3.7	*Cat.*, *Soph. El.*, *Gener. An.* I, *Metaph.* I, *Pol.* V
3.6	*Top.* II, *Phys.* I, III, *Metaph.* Z, *Mech.*
3.5	*Int.*, *Top.* III, VII, *Cael.* II, *Virt.*, *Insomn.*, *Col.*
3.4	*Phys.* VI, VII, *Cael.* I, *Mete.* I, *Metaph.* N, *Pol.* VIII
3.3	*Metaph.* A, B, M, *Pol.* III
3.2	*Metaph.* Γ, *EE* VIII
3.1	*Aud.*
3.0	*MM*, *EE* I, *Rhet.* II
2.9	
2.8	*An.* III
2.7	*Top.* V, VI, *Div. Somn.*
2.6	*Top.* IV, *Epist.*
2.5	*Protrept.*

Values between n.m0 and n.m9 appear on the line marked n.m.

Protrepticus which, whatever its substantial authenticity, does not come to us as the unedited work of Aristotle. Apart from *Mete.*, none of the other dubious works under consideration here appears out of line with the main body of the genuine texts.

In respect of γάρ, shown in Table 11.5, the only one of our five works to stand out is *Metaph.* α. Its value, 3.01, is higher than any except *Top.* Δ (3.04), *Long.* (3.01) and *EN* VIII (3.35). But though its

Table 11.5. *Proportion of* γάρ *in works of Aristotle*

3.3	*EN* VIII
3.2	
3.1	
3.0	*Top.* IV, *Metaph.* α, *Long.*
2.9	
2.8	*Top.* VI, *EN* IV, *Epist.*
2.7	
2.6	*Phys.* VI, *EE* I, *Rhet.* II
2.5	*Cat.*, *EN* IX, X
2.4	*Top.* II, VII, *Phys.* III, *EN* VI, *MM*, *Rhet.* III
2.3	*Top.* III, *Phys.* V, VII, VIII, *Gener. Corr.* II, *Metaph.* Z, Λ, *EN* III, *Div. Somn.*
2.2	*Top.* V, VIII, *Cael.* I, II, III, *Gener. Corr.* I, *Metaph.* B, Γ, Θ, K, *EN* I, *EE* III, *Pol.* I, *Rhet.* I
2.1	*Top.* I, IX, *Phys.* I, IV, *Mete.* II, *Gener. An.* III, *Metaph.* M, *Spir.*, *Aud.*
2.0	*Anal. Post.* I, II, *An.* I, *Part. An.*, *Gener. An.* IV–V, *Metaph.* E, I, *EN* V, VII, *EE* I, *Pol.* II, V, *Respir.*, *Lin.*
1.9	*Anal. Pr.* II, *Mete.* III, *An.* II, *Gener. An.* I, II, *EE* VIII, *Pol.* III, VII, *Col.*
1.8	*Int.*, *Anal. Pr.* I, *Mete.* IV, *An.* III, *Metaph.* A, *EE* II, *Pol.* VIII, *Somn.*
1.7	*Phys.* II, *Cael.* IV, *Mot. An.*, *Inc. An.*, *EN* II, *Pol.* VI, *Juv.*, *Mech.*, *Protrept.*
1.6	*Mete.* I, *Pol.* IV, *Insomn.*, *Vent.*
1.5	*Metaph.* Δ, N
1.4	*Metaph.* H
1.3	
1.2	
1.1	
1.0	
0.9	
0.8	
0.7	
0.6	*Ath. Pol.*
0.5–	*Virt.*

value is high it is, as will be seen, in quite good company; this is the first case where one apex of the distribution is occupied by works commonly assumed genuine. At the other end we have the spurious *Virt.* and the controverted *Ath. Pol.*

Finally we may look at the overall distribution of μέν (Table 11.6). Again *Mete.* IV stands at an extreme point, with the second

Table 11.6. *Proportion of μέν in works of Aristotle*

3.0	
2.9	
2.8	
2.7	
2.6	
2.5	*EN* II
2.4	
2.3	*Mete.* IV
2.2	*Cael.* IV, *Gener. Corr.* I
2.1	*Gener. Corr.* II, *Gener. An.* IV–V, *EN* VII, *Pol.* I, IV
2.0	*Juv.*
1.9	*Gener. An.* III, *Metaph.* A, *Pol.* VI, *Respir.*
1.8	*Anal. Pr.* I, II, *Cael.* III, *An.* II, *Part. An., Mot. An., Inc. An., Gener. An.* II, *EE* III
1.7	*Anal. Post.* I, *Phys.* I, V, VIII, *Mete.* III, *EN* V, *EE* I, II, VII, *Pol.* II, III, VII, *Long., Epist.*
1.6	*Top.* I, *Phys.* IV, *Mete.* I, II, *Gener. An.* I, *Metaph.* Δ, E, Z, Θ, *EN* III, VI, *Pol.* V, *Rhet.* I, *Somn., Ath. Pol.*
1.5	*Int., Top.* VII, VIII, *Soph. El., Phys.* II, *Cael.* II, *An.* III, *Metaph.* B, H, M, *EE* VIII
1.4	*Anal. Post.* II, *Top.* V, *Phys.* III, *Metaph.* α, I, Λ, *EN* IV, VIII, *Rhet.* III, *Insomn., Mech., Vent.*
1.3	*Cat., Top.* II, III, *Phys.* VII, *An.* I, *Metaph.* N, *EN* I
1.2	*Cael.* I, *Metaph.* K, *EN* IX, *MM, Pol.* VIII, *Col.*
1.1	*Phys.* VI, *Metaph.* Γ, *Rhet.* II, *Protrept.*
1.0	*Top.* VI, *EN* X, *Aud.*
0.9	*Top.* IV, *Virt., Spir., Lin.*
0.8	
0.7	
0.6	*Div. Somn.*
0.5	
0.4	
0.3	

highest value of the hundred texts; again the value cannot be regarded as intolerably high in itself, since it is surpassed by that of the highly respectable second book of *EN*. Again, the other end of the scale is occupied principally by works of low repute, such as *Virt.*, *Spir.* and *Lin.*

The overall picture to emerge from these four tables is this. Against the background of the general variability in Aristotle's use of these particles, the usage in *Cat.*, *Mot. An.* and *Metaph.* K is not such as to allow any argument to be brought on this ground against their authenticity. But *Mete.* IV occupies in the distributions for καί and μέν and δέ a point sufficient extreme to arouse suspicion; and so does *Metaph.* α in the distributions for καί and γάρ. Other books of unquestioned authenticity occupy extreme points in one or other distribution; but very few do so more than once. (The exceptions are *EN* II, καί and μέν; *Top.* IV, δέ, γάρ, μέν.)

II

I now turn to consider the usage of twenty other particles and connectives, less frequent than the four so far considered. It will be useful to begin by concentrating on the two disputed books from *Metaph.* and considering them in comparison with the rest of *Metaph*, rather than against the background of the entire corpus. Table 11.7 sets out the occurrences of these twenty particles, in addition to the four already considered, in each of the books of *Metaph.* Table 11.8 gives the corresponding relative frequency and standard error for each particle in each book. (Beneath each particle is given in brackets its relative frequency in the large corpus of 291,588 words.) What can these tables tell us about the authenticity of α and K?

The first thing which the tables give is a warning about the limitations of our method. It will be seen that book Δ often diverges from the general pattern of particle usage. Indeed, if we take the *Metaphysics* as a whole as a population and ask, in respect of each particle in turn, whether Δ can be regarded as a random sample drawn from it, we find that in no less than thirteen of the twenty-four cases in the list the Δ frequencies exhibit a statistically significant difference from the population frequency. The reason for this is not that Δ is inauthentic, but that it is a

Table 11.7.

Metaph	A	α	B	Γ	Δ	E	Z	H	Θ	I	K	Λ	M	N
ἀλλά	66	17	58	83	58	26	117	30	49	59	44	64	72	59
ἄν	59	10	49	62	53	11	50	10	21	21	53	24	39	25
γάρ	150	35	117	149	138	38	219	41	98	105	159	117	169	73
γε	20	5	19	27	5	4	22	1	11	7	16	15	21	18
δέ	266	45	176	215	356	70	334	124	181	194	317	200	271	164
δή	17	1	6	13	15	3	26	17	18	17	19	20	20	18
διό	11	5	3	8	19	3	19	3	12	19	8	2	5	5
εἰ	40	8	78	101	24	19	87	22	39	36	77	50	104	46
ἐπεί	7	1	1	12	9	7	19	6	10	9	18	13	16	8
ἤ	73	10	81	108	226	42	174	44	82	112	125	73	89	55
καθάπερ	8	2	4	5	0	0	4	2	1	3	8	0	3	3
καί	472	41	285	389	543	82	543	176	266	304	346	294	472	273
μέν	155	17	82	76	145	30	155	45	71	77	92	74	128	66
μή	40	17	42	107	93	16	69	16	72	37	76	42	62	53
οἷον	34	7	25	17	124	10	93	34	35	32	30	28	38	19
ὅτι	44	3	22	80	67	21	81	25	37	43	39	31	48	40
οὐ	76	29	65	149	84	30	173	41	87	80	131	74	111	66
οὐδέ	21	12	32	16	10	11	55	19	25	16	37	19	28	18
οὖν	52	2	21	32	26	9	45	10	18	15	24	24	32	26
οὔτε	45	4	16	30	11	9	26	8	8	18	47	13	41	27
τε	57	4	49	23	30	1	35	12	7	18	23	26	41	25
ὡς	52	10	23	25	79	31	62	27	22	40	22	40	51	32
ὥσπερ	28	2	9	20	25	1	41	13	10	26	8	15	27	19
ὥστε	15	7	21	35	15	8	42	6	19	32	33	16	42	10
Total number of words	8,029	1,162	5,281	6,575	8,857	1,820	9,188	2,835	4,421	5,215	7,132	5,077	8,033	4,729

Table 11.8. *Aristotle's Metaphysics: particles in individual books*

Particle	A	α	B	Γ	Δ	E	Z	H	Θ	I	K	Λ	M	N
ἀλλά	0.82	1.46	1.10	1.26	0.65	1.43	1.26	1.06	1.11	1.13	0.62	1.26	0.90	1.29
(0.90)	.10	.35	.14	.15	.09	.28	.12	.19	.16	.15	.09	.16	.11	.16
ἄν	0.73	0.86	0.93	0.94	0.60	0.60	0.54	0.35	0.48	0.73	0.74	0.47	0.49	0.53
(0.64)	.10	.27	.13	.12	.08	.18	.08	.11	.10	.12	.10	.10	.08	.11
γάρ	1.87	3.01	2.22	2.27	1.56	2.09	2.36	1.45	2.22	2.01	2.23	2.30	2.10	1.55
(2.16)	.15	.50	.20	.18	.13	.34	.16	.22	.22	.20	.17	.21	.16	.18
γε	0.25	0.43	0.36	0.41	0.06	0.22	0.24	0.04	0.25	0.13	0.22	0.30	0.26	0.38
(0.17)	.06	.19	.08	.08	.03	.11	.05	.04	.07	.05	.06	.08	.06	.09
δέ	3.31	3.87	3.33	3.27	4.02	3.85	3.60	4.37	4.09	3.72	4.44	3.94	3.37	3.47
(4.00)	.20	.57	.25	.22	.21	.45	.19	.38	.30	.27	.24	.27	.20	.27
δή	0.21	0.09	0.11	0.20	0.17	0.16	0.28	0.60	0.41	0.33	0.27	0.39	0.25	0.38
(0.26)	.05	.09	.05	.05	.04	.10	.05	.14	.10	.08	.06	.09	.06	.09
διό	0.14	0.43	0.06	0.12	0.21	0.16	0.20	0.11	0.27	0.36	0.11	0.04	0.04	0.11
(0.20)	.04	.19	.03	.04	.05	.10	.05	.06	.08	.08	.04	.03	.02	.05
εἰ	0.50	0.69	1.48	1.54	0.27	1.04	0.94	0.78	0.88	0.69	1.08	0.98	1.29	0.97
(0.65)	.08	.24	.17	.15	.06	.24	.10	.16	.14	.12	.12	.14	.13	.14
ἐπεί	0.09	0.09	0.02	0.18	0.10	0.38	0.20	0.21	0.23	0.17	0.25	0.26	0.20	0.17
(0.17)	.03	.09	.02	.05	.03	.15	.05	.09	.07	.06	.06	.07	.05	.06
ἤ	0.91	0.86	1.53	1.64	2.55	2.31	1.87	1.55	1.85	2.44	1.75	1.44	1.11	1.16
(1.47)	.11	.27	.17	.16	.17	.35	.14	.23	.20	.21	.16	.17	.12	.16
καθάπερ	0.10	0.17	0.08	0.08	0.00	0.00	0.04	0.07	0.02	0.06	0.11	0.00	0.04	0.06
(0.09)	.04	.12	.04	.03	.00	.00	.02	.05	.02	.03	.04	.00	.02	.04
καί	5.88	3.53	5.40	5.92	6.13	4.51	5.85	6.21	6.02	5.83	4.85	5.79	5.87	5.77
(6.00)	.26	.54	.31	.29	.25	.49	.24	.45	.36	.33	.25	.33	.26	.35

μέν	1.93	1.46	1.55	1.16	1.64	1.65	1.67	1.59	1.61	1.48	1.29	1.46	1.59	1.39
(1.62)	.15	.35	.17	.13	.13	.30	.13	.23	.19	.17	.13	.17	.14	.17
μή	0.50	1.46	0.80	1.63	1.05	0.88	0.74	0.56	1.63	0.71	1.07	0.83	0.77	1.12
(0.82)	.08	.35	.12	.16	.11	.22	.09	.14	.19	.12	.12	.13	.10	.15
οἷον	0.43	0.60	0.47	0.26	1.40	0.55	1.00	1.20	0.79	0.61	0.42	0.55	0.47	0.40
(0.51)	.07	.23	.09	.06	.12	.17	.10	.20	.13	.11	.08	.10	.08	.09
ὅτι	0.55	0.26	0.42	1.22	0.76	1.15	0.87	0.88	0.84	0.82	0.55	0.61	0.60	0.84
(0.68)	.08	.15	.09	.14	.09	.25	.10	.18	.14	.13	.09	.11	.09	.13
οὖ	0.95	2.50	1.23	2.27	0.95	1.65	1.86	1.45	1.97	1.53	1.84	1.46	1.38	1.39
(1.29)	.11	.46	.15	.18	.10	.30	.14	.22	.21	.17	.16	.17	.13	.17
οὐδέ	0.26	1.03	0.61	0.24	0.11	0.60	0.59	0.67	0.57	0.31	0.52	0.37	0.35	0.38
(0.34)	.06	.30	.11	.06	.04	.18	.08	.15	.11	.08	.09	.09	.07	.09
οὖν	0.65	0.17	0.40	0.49	0.29	0.49	0.48	0.35	0.41	0.29	0.34	0.47	0.40	0.55
(0.45)	.09	.12	.09	.09	.06	.16	.07	.11	.10	.07	.07	.10	.07	.11
οὔτε	0.56	0.34	0.30	0.46	0.12	0.49	0.28	0.28	0.18	0.35	0.66	0.26	0.51	0.57
(0.26)	.08	.17	.08	.08	.04	.16	.05	.10	.06	.08	.10	.07	.08	.11
τε	0.71	0.34	0.93	0.35	0.34	0.05	0.38	0.42	0.16	0.35	0.32	0.51	0.51	0.53
(0.52)	.09	.17	.13	.07	.06	.05	.06	.12	.06	.08	.07	.10	.08	.11
ὡς	0.65	0.86	0.44	0.38	0.89	1.70	0.67	0.95	0.50	0.77	0.31	0.79	0.63	0.68
(0.53)	.09	.27	.09	.08	.10	.30	.08	.18	.11	.12	.07	.12	.09	.12
ὥσπερ	0.35	0.17	0.17	0.30	0.28	0.05	0.44	0.46	0.23	0.50	0.11	0.30	0.34	0.40
(0.34)	.07	.12	.06	.07	.06	.05	.07	.13	.07	.11	.04	.08	.06	.09
ὥστε	0.19	0.60	0.40	0.53	0.17	0.44	0.45	0.28	0.43	0.61	0.46	0.32	0.52	0.21
(0.29)	.05	.23	.09	.09	.04	.16	.07	.10	.10	.11	.08	.08	.08	.07

different kind of work from the rest of *Metaph.*, being a dictionary or lexicon of philosophical terms. Hence, particles frequent in argumentative writing (e.g. εἰ) score low; whereas particles for introducing examples, such as οἷον, score high. This illustrates how genre may be at least as important as authorship or chronology in determining the distribution of particles in a work. It can only be safe to draw arguments about the attribution of texts from the distribution of their particles in cases where the texts are clearly of the same genre (as are, for instance, *EN* and *EE*).

From the figures given in Tables 11.7 and 11.8 we can work out the average frequency for each particle in the whole *Metaphysics*; and we can ask, of each book, with respect to each particle, whether it displays a value to be expected of a random sample drawn from the total population constituted by *Metaph.* We can calculate which divergences from the population proportion are unlikely to occur by chance more than once in a hundred times: we call these divergences which are statistically significant at the 1 per cent level. We can then ask how many such divergences occur in the case of each book.

If we ask this question, we find that neither α nor K stand out uniquely from the other books of the *Metaphysics*. In α there are three divergences significant at the 1% level: those in the use of καί, of οὐ, and of οὐδέ. In K there are eight such divergences: ἀλλά, δέ, καί, οἷον, οὔτε, τε, ὡζ and ὥσπερ. But there are a greater number of statistically significant divergences in the case of books A (9), and Γ (10). B has 5 divergences, and all the other books have four or less (EZHΘIΛMN). Book α, therefore, does not stand out from the others if we take this approach. This is not because the frequencies it exhibits are particularly close to the overall proportions; it is because it is so short that its standard errors are high and it takes a large divergence to be statistically significant.

A different picture emerges if we take the particles not one by one, but all together. We can correlate the usage of all twenty of the newly introduced particles in a book with the usage in another book, to see how closely the overall pattern in the first book resembles that in the second. The product-moment coefficient of correlation, as it is called, provides a measure of similarity between books thus compared: if two books have a correlation coefficient of 1 they resemble each other totally in respect of the feature compared; if they have a coefficient of 0 they are totally dissimilar. Obviously any two books written in Greek are likely to resemble each other to some extent in respect of particle usage: that is to say, if we are comparing the use of twenty items the books can be expected to have a coefficient value of more than one-half. (It can be calculated that a correlation of more than 0.54 is extremely unlikely to have come about by chance.) Figure 11.1 sets out the correlation, in respect of these twenty particles, between each book of *Metaph*, and each other book: the correlations are exhibited in a matrix of the kind used in road-atlases to represent the distances between pairs of towns.

It will be seen that the great majority of correlations are high. A correlation of 0.65 has only one chance in a thousand of being the result of mere chance resemblance. If we read the diagram from right to left we do not come upon a correlation which is lower than this until we reach the column for Γ: here we find that the correlations with H and with Δ are below this level. Only Δ in the column for B is below it, and in the column for A only the correlations with Δ, Θ, and α. But six items in the column for α fall below the level. So that of the eleven correlations in the whole matrix which fall below the level of 0.65, seven are correlations involving α. It will be noticed also that the remaining values in the α column are between 0.65 and 0.70. In the case of every other book the majority of correlations are above 0.70.

The impression that α stands out on its own is confirmed if we add to the twenty particles introduced in the present section the four common particles studied earlier. Figure 11.2 sets out the correlation matrix for all the books for all twenty-four particles. It leaps to the eye that α stands alone. Every correlation not involving α is higher than 0.9, and the great majority are over 0.95; no correlation involving α is higher than 0.85.

III

We now turn from the dubious *Metaphysics* books to the other three objects of our study. Table 11.9 sets out the occurrences, relative frequencies, and standard errors for the twenty particles in each of these books: for comparison there is added the proportion and standard error for each particle in the large sample consisting of the *Metaphysics, Ethics, An., Pol.* and *Rhet*. I shall

Values of R

	A	α	B	Γ	Δ	E	Z	H	Θ	I	K	Λ	M	N
A	1.00													
α	0.57	1.00												
B	0.75	0.51	1.00											
Γ	0.69	0.65	0.80	1.00										
Δ	0.63	0.35	0.62	0.58	1.00									
E	0.72	0.49	0.72	0.72	0.79	1.00								
Z	0.76	0.68	0.79	0.80	0.81	0.85	1.00							
H	0.67	0.48	0.65	0.59	0.84	0.83	0.91	1.00						
Θ	0.64	0.70	0.74	0.88	0.80	0.79	0.90	0.79	1.00					
I	0.73	0.52	0.76	0.75	0.87	0.88	0.91	0.83	0.85	1.00				
K	0.69	0.69	0.82	0.88	0.70	0.75	0.85	0.68	0.89	0.84	1.00			
Λ	0.82	0.68	0.85	0.85	0.71	0.86	0.93	0.84	0.88	0.85	0.82	1.00		
M	0.76	0.65	0.88	0.89	0.59	0.78	0.86	0.72	0.81	0.77	0.87	0.92	1.00	
N	0.83	0.63	0.80	0.91	0.65	0.81	0.85	0.74	0.87	0.78	0.81	0.94	0.90	1.00

Figure 11.1. Correlation matrix for twenty particles between books of Metaph.

Values of R

	A	α	B	Γ	Δ	E	Z	H	Θ	I	K	Λ	M	N
A	1.00													
α	0.78	1.00												
B	0.97	0.81	1.00											
Γ	0.94	0.82	0.97	1.00										
Δ	0.95	0.75	0.94	0.92	1.00									
E	0.91	0.82	0.93	0.91	0.94	1.00								
Z	0.97	0.84	0.98	0.97	0.97	0.95	1.00							
H	0.96	0.78	0.95	0.93	0.98	0.94	0.98	1.00						
Θ	0.95	0.85	0.97	0.97	0.97	0.95	0.99	0.97	1.00					
I	0.96	0.80	0.97	0.96	0.98	0.96	0.99	0.98	0.98	1.00				
K	0.93	0.88	0.96	0.95	0.94	0.94	0.96	0.94	0.97	0.96	1.00			
Λ	0.98	0.85	0.98	0.97	0.96	0.95	0.99	0.98	0.98	0.98	0.97	1.00		
M	0.98	0.81	0.98	0.97	0.94	0.92	0.98	0.97	0.97	0.97	0.96	0.99	1.00	
N	0.98	0.79	0.97	0.97	0.95	0.93	0.98	0.98	0.98	0.97	0.95	0.99	0.99	1.00
	A	α	B	Γ	Δ	E	Z	H	Θ	I	K	Λ	M	N

Figure 11.2. Correlation matrix for twenty-four particles between books of *Metaph.*

Table 11.9. *Twenty particles in some dubious works of Aristotle*

Particle	Cat.			Mete. IV			Mot. An.			Large sample	
	No.	%	SE	No.	%	SE	No.	%	SE	%	SE
ἀλλά	48	0.45	0.07	48	0.63	0.09	22	0.53	0.11	0.90	0.02
ἄν	64	0.63	0.08	22	0.29	0.06	26	0.63	0.12	0.64	0.02
γε	49	0.48	0.07	3	0.04	0.02	2	0.05	0.03	0.17	0.01
δή	2	0.02	0.01	8	0.11	0.04	2	0.05	0.03	0.26	0.01
διό	1	0.01	0.01	30	0.40	0.07	7	0.17	0.06	0.20	0.01
εἰ	46	0.45	0.07	17	0.22	0.05	32	0.78	0.13	0.65	0.01
ἐπεί	2	0.02	0.01	17	0.22	0.05	6	0.15	0.06	0.17	0.01
ἤ	155	1.52	0.12	148	1.95	0.16	46	1.12	0.16	1.47	0.02
καθάπερ	3	0.03	0.02	3	0.04	0.03	1	0.02	0.02	0.09	0.01
μή	73	0.71	0.03	52	0.69	0.10	25	0.61	0.12	0.82	0.02
οἷον	116	1.13	0.10	93	1.23	0.12	16	0.39	0.10	0.51	0.01
ὅτι	37	0.36	0.06	24	0.32	0.06	24	0.58	0.12	0.68	0.02
οὐ	87	0.85	0.09	84	1.11	0.12	35	0.85	0.14	1.29	0.02
οὐδέ	37	0.36	0.06	9	0.12	0.04	9	0.22	0.07	0.34	0.01
οὖν	33	0.32	0.06	55	0.73	0.10	23	0.56	0.11	0.45	0.01
οὔτε	55	0.53	0.07	18	0.24	0.05	4	0.10	0.05	0.26	0.01
τε	41	0.40	0.06	14	0.18	0.05	18	0.44	0.10	0.52	0.01
ὡς	42	0.41	0.06	26	0.34	0.06	13	0.32	0.09	0.53	0.01
ὥσπερ	5	0.05	0.02	37	0.49	0.08	19	0.46	0.11	0.34	0.01
ὥστε	51	0.49	0.07	32	0.42	0.07	20	0.49	0.11	0.29	0.01
Total words in book	10,213			7,585			4,120			291,588	

For each book is given first the absolute number of occurrences of the particle, followed by the proportion in per cent, followed by the appropriate standard error. The large sample used as a yardstick for comparison consists of *Metaph.*, *EN*, *EE*, *An.*, *Pol.* and *Rhet.* in their entireties.

compare each of the dubious works in turn with the values in the sample as a whole and the values in the individual forty-three books which make it up.

First, the *Categories*. The values for ἄν, ἤ, καθάπερ, μή, οὐδέ, οὖν, τε, ὡς do not differ significantly from those in the large sample. ἀλλά is significantly low at 0.46; it is also lower, as can be seen from Table 11.8, than any recorded in *Metaph.* It is in fact lower than anything recorded in any of the individual books making up the large sample with the exception of *EN* IX (0.42). γε is significantly high, at 0.48. No book in any of the works making up the sample surpasses it; the nearest to it is the value in α (0.45). δή is significantly low at 0.02; it is lower than any book in the sample. διό too is significantly low: only *EE* I, which has no occurrence of the particle, is lower than its value of 0.01. εἰ is significantly low, but its value is within the range recorded in *Metaph.*; this is a particle whose value fluctuates greatly in Aristotelian texts. The same can be said of ἐπεί, also significantly low but not lower than *Metaph.* B or several books of *EN.* οἷον is significantly high, but within the range of variation in *Metaph.* ὅτι at 0.36 is significantly low, and lower than anything in *Metaph*, except the dubious α; elsewhere only *EN* IV and VIII and four books of *Pol.* are lower. ου οὔτε is high at 0.53, but is surpassed thrice in *Metaph.* ὥσπερ, significantly low at 0.05, is matched elsewhere only by *Metaph.* E. On the basis of the comparison with the forty-three book sample, then, we can say that *Cat*, is eccentric in its low values of ἀλλά, δή, διό, ὥσπερ; and in its high values of γε.

In the case of *Mete.* IV we find that there are no significant differences from the sample proportions in the case of ἐπεί, καθάπερ, μή, οὐ, οὔτε, ὥσπερ and ὥστε. ἀλλά is low, but not as low as *Cat.* or as half a dozen other books in the sample. ἄν, on the other hand, at 0.29 is lower than any other book in the sample. γε is low at 0.04, but paralleled by *Metaph.* H; no other book scores quite as low. δή is low at 0.11, but there are half a dozen books lower. διό on the other hand is the highest recorded except for *EE* VIII (0.41). In the case of εἰ, ἤ, and οἷον the differences from the sample proportion are statistically significant, but the values recorded are within the wide range of fluctuation characteristic of Aristotle's use of these particles. ὅτι is significantly low, lower than in *Cat.*; but again *EN* IV and VIII and four books of *Pol.* are lower. οὐδέ, τε, and ὡς diverge significantly from the sample proportion, but they are within the range of variation in *Metaph.* οὖν, at 0.73, is high; but it is matched by two books in *EN*, and is closely approximated by *Mete.* III itself (0.71). Only ἄν, γε, and διό of these particles therefore display a degree of eccentricity sufficient to arouse suspicion.

Fourteen out of the twenty particles in *Mot. Anim.* occur at a rate which shows no significant difference from the sample proportion. The exceptions are as follows. ἀλλά is low; but *EN* IX and X are both lower, as is *Cat.* γε is low, but not as low as *Mete.* IV or *Metaph.* H, and is paralleled by *Rhet.* I. The low καθάπερ is paralleled by half a dozen books in the sample, and οὐ is within the fluctuations characteristic of it. The low οὔτε, unparalleled in *Metaph.*, is surpassed by *EN* VIII, IX, X and by two books of *Rhet.* Nothing here therefore, except possibly the low ἀλλά, really gives ground for suspicion of the authenticity of the treatise.

The overall conclusion, then, of this study is as follows. We have discovered in our examination of twenty-four particles no real evidence suggesting the spuriousness of *Metaph.* K or of *Mot. Anim.* But the frequencies of ἀλλά, δή, διό, ὥσπερ, and γε in *Cat.* and of καί, μέν, δέ, ἄν, γε, διό in *Mete.* IV are eccentric enough to be suspicious. And the overall picture of particle usage in *Metaph.* α appears to be quite different from that in other works of Aristotle.

Index